The **Cringe** Chronicles

Mortifying Misadventures with My Dad:

A Memoir

Kristin Tougias & Michael J. Tougias

To Dottie & Daughter Rita

Best Wishes
MJ Tougias

BLACK ROSE
writing™

The final approval for this literary material is granted by the author.

First printing

All stories, events, and people are true. Some names, locations and dates have been changed to protect the guilty.

ISBN: 978-1-61296-340-2

PUBLISHED BY BLACK ROSE WRITING

www.blackrosewriting.com

Printed in the United States of America

The Cringe Chronicles is printed in Cambria

DEDICATION

To my incredibly wonderful Mom and brother, for always

supporting and putting up with me. And to my Dad, for making me

want the unconventional for myself (after my early teen years

chronicled in this book, that is). And for empowering me with

knowledge, trust, guidance and love every day of my life. I am so

grateful to be your daughter. –K.T.

The Cringe Chronicles

Mortifying Misadventures with My Dad:

A Memoir

CONTENTS

CHAPTER 1   THE FAMILY VACATION FROM HELL   7

CHAPTER 2   THE FIRST DAY IS THE WORST DAY   34

CHAPTER 3   A LOSING SEASON   53

CHAPTER 4   THE SHARK ENCOUNTER   76

CHAPTER 5   THE FIRST JOB - "SERVE THE F'N ICE CREAM"   88

CHAPTER 6   MY FREE WEEKEND AT THE OUTHOUSE   118

CHAPTER 7   A DAD AND GRAD ABROAD   132

CHAPTER 1

THE FAMILY VACATION FROM HELL

"I've got good news everyone!" my father shouted. "We've been offered a free weekend at a place in New Hampshire called North Lake Resort. They're giving us a cottage to stay in, food is included, and there are plenty of activities."

I didn't like the sound of this. My Dad was a travel writer and was often offered free trips in exchange for an article in his newspaper column featuring the place in which he stayed. Sometimes the free trip was fun, sometimes it was a nightmare, so I had to be wary.

It was Monday afternoon, and we were in the kitchen with my mother. "When," she asked, while scrubbing a dried spaghetti noodle off the surface of a white plate, "is the weekend at this lake?"

"Why it's this weekend!" my Dad said as he threw his arms up into the air triumphantly before continuing. "We're going to have a great time."

Then he did something annoying. He did a little dance, kind of like an Irish jig. When I didn't say anything in response to this "great news" he looked at me and said, "And do you know why we're going to have such a good time?"

I looked at him blankly and shook my head. "Because it's free!" he bellowed. "How can we not have a good time when we don't have to spend a dime!"

I started to walk upstairs to my room when it hit me. *Oh no. Not this weekend—Jess's pool party is this weekend!*

I ran back into the kitchen to find my father meticulously studying a large map of New Hampshire.

"Dad, I can't go. At least not this weekend."

"What? Of course you can go. Kristin, you love lakes. You love the mountains. It's a once in a lifetime trip."

"Mom!" I screamed out of desperation. "This weekend is Jess's pool party!"

My father glared at my mother, and I did the same. She had managed to scrape the crusted noodle off the plate's surface, and was now glancing back and forth between us. Then, looking at me, she said, "Kristin, we'll figure something out..." But I knew the decision had already been made.

* * *

It was the summer before ninth grade and my first year of high school, and I was glad for the three month respite from classes, teachers, homework, and fellow students. My last year of middle school had been a difficult one, especially for my social life or what little there was of it. Eighth graders didn't do the things they wanted to do. They did what others wanted them to do, because as a teenager the social world rules above all, and it's survival of the coolest.

Acceptance among peers is crucial; yet obtaining this acceptance was a challenge for me. That is why over the summer I needed to solidify my ties with the "in crowd" to ensure my success in high school, but things had a way of not working out for me when I needed them to. For example, just twenty or so years ago the kid with braces endured harsh jokes for having a metal mouth. But now it seemed every 14-year-old had braces, many multi-colored, while I was the only one to expose naked teeth. And mine were far from perfect with a large space protruding between my two front teeth that my dentist believed would correct itself over time with no need for braces. He explained that as my molars and wisdom teeth grew in, the space that "you could drive a boat between"—according to my brother—would close on its own in a couple years. So while the other kids had brackets and bars to fix their teeth within months, I was looking at an incredibly long time —years—for mine to self-correct. And time, measured in years, isn't good enough when you're judged on a daily basis.

* * *

A few days after my father announced the free trip, I found myself in the car heading to New Hampshire. My Dad's car was an old green Subaru wagon, so unkempt it supported many other forms of life. All my friend's parents had one regular sized car, and then a larger SUV type, neither of which looked like the small, beat-up Subaru we had. Every time my father drove my friends and I to a dance or to the movies, I dreaded the moment my friends would step foot in the car and be choked by its terrible stench.

The Subaru had the constant smell of sweaty hiking shoes, moldy evergreen trees, and fish. Before sitting down you had to wipe away the twigs, peanuts and dirt sprinkled across the seat. A large spider had taken up residence in the car, and about every third trip I made in the Subaru, it would emerge from a dark corner, often when I had friends riding with me. When I tried to kill it the first time I saw it, my father screamed, "Don't hurt it, it's become like a pet to me." And he was serious.

The car was like a nature museum on wheels, and I hated it. Or more to the point, I hated how there was nothing I could do about it. I would implore my Dad to get a new car, or at the least try to keep his clean and get rid of the putrid smell. He would respond by invariably saying, "I live in this car Kristin!" or, "you know how hard I work!" And it was true, my Dad did work long hours, going into Boston each weekday to his job at the insurance company and either writing or giving presentations about his books at night. On the nights when he had a presentation he'd leave his office at 5 p.m. and eat dinner in the car while driving to his speaking location, holding the wheel in one hand and his food in the other so that half of it almost always rolled down between the seats where it eventually solidified.

To make matters worse, my father went fishing in his free time, usually laying his catch on the floor mats until he got home. The Subaru's conditions were gruesome to me, but embarrassing more than anything. And to top it off, my Dad's clothes were as bad as his car, so it was not unusual to see him driving the ancient green wagon wearing green short-shorts with a pink and turquoise striped polo-shirt. And no, he is not colorblind. He actually thinks the outfit is stylish and doesn't realize that just making eye contact with that color combo sends a piercing pain through the eyeballs.

The whole way to New Hampshire I was not talking, and I was not happy. This was the day of Jess's pool party and I was missing the social highlight of the entire summer. Now I would be one crucial pool party behind the rest of the girls in my grade, and I would have to establish myself at some other gathering. But this was a long shot in itself, for only two weeks of summer remained. I had hoped the summer would be my chance to improve my social standing, but so far it was a complete failure.

My younger brother Brian asked me why I wasn't talking, even though he knew the reason. Brian was three years younger than me, yet ten times more immature. We got along most of the time, but a four-hour car ride almost guaranteed conflict.

"Kristin's not talking to me," Brian whined to my parents. "And she's hogging most of the back seat. I don't have any room." There wasn't much of a back seat to hog, because whenever we traveled my Dad put a large light blue cooler between us, taking up more room than a person. The cooler was from the Middle Ages, and it was gross. It even had a little blood on the outside of it; probably from the few fish my father didn't throw on the floor mat but took the time to put on ice. My mother had asked him to buy a new one, and so had I—many times. But he always said the same thing; "It still works fine, so we don't need a new one."

I'm not sure whether the cooler was put in that spot to separate my brother and me, or if it was simply the only space left for it, but it made me feel cramped. No—trapped. Not only was my body jammed between the car door and the cooler, but I had two fishing poles protruding along both sides of my head that often became tangled in my hair whenever I attempted to adjust myself in the tiny space allotted. Simply put, this green rust bucket of a car was jam-packed, and 90 percent of the stuff was my father's. There were paddles, maps, life jackets, tackle boxes, nets and all sorts of junk in the back. You would think we were packing up and moving to live on a river in the Yukon. A canoe, a kayak, and even an old set of golf clubs were lashed to the roof rack on top of the car. I prayed no one had seen us as we left town.

We looked ridiculous, resembling a bunch of Hillbillies wedged in a jalopy, making our first foray down from the hills. And now we were heading to the middle of nowhere, and I was going to miss the best pool party of the year. Truth be told, it was the first party I'd been invited to in a long time. And it was definitely the first summer party with boys.

* * *

It was a long ride to North Lake, but once we were out of our home state of Massachusetts, I decided to start talking again. I asked my father what this place we were staying at would be like.

"Well," he said, turning off the bizarre folk music emitting from the radio, "it's a lake resort. And a good one too. There's all sorts of stuff to do there. They have basketball courts and mini-golf for your brother, good fishing for me, and a nice beach for you and Mom."

It was 2 p.m. and I was starving, since all we had had to eat in the car were potato chips and apples. My father had made sandwiches but the rest of us wouldn't eat them. They were "tomato sandwiches" and the juice from the tomatoes made the bread soggy. My father ate three, saying, "I grew these tomatoes, and they're organic. You guys eat too much processed stuff. All those chemicals are going to kill you, so don't come crying to me when you get cancer" while he cheerfully bopped his head to the beat of the folk music. Brian leaned over the cooler and whispered to me, "Dad made me a sandwich one time for school this year. It was a carrot and mustard sandwich. I almost puked." I made an empathetic scowl face followed by a silent barfing imitation that made him laugh.

When we got off the highway, the roads became narrower as we left civilization behind. My mother made my father stop at a lone gas station where Brian and I bought candy bars before we continued driving the back roads. After about another hour of driving we saw a sign that read, "North Lake Resort—Come Stay Awhile." The sign, held up by wooden poles suspended over a dirt lane, was hand carved and painted red and white. My father turned right and we rattled down the uneven lane that was barely wider than the car. I thought the canoe and kayak strapped above would shake loose and go airborne, and if that happened my father would go ballistic and make a scene. Fortunately we made it out of the gloomy woods without incident and entered into a clearing where we stopped in front of a small white building. A plastic sign above the building's only door said "Main Office". My Dad went inside, while my mother, Brian and I waited silently in the car. The three of us peered out the windows, and my brother said, "What are those?" I knew he was looking at the tiny, shiny metal trailer homes that I too was examining.

"Probably where the staff lives," my Mom said.

"What's the staff?" asked Brian.

"You know, the people that work here."

After another minute my father came out of the office with a set of keys in hand. Hopping back in the car, he said, "We're in lucky number seven."

We drove further down the dirt lane. Brian and I were fighting to lean over the cooler in an effort to get the first look at our cottage through the front window. But the car suddenly turned left, and out in front of us was a gleaming metal box-shaped mobile home. As dread engulfed me and pure confusion swallowed Brian, we all stared silently at the sign on the door that read "7".

"Oh my God," I blurted out, "This can't be where we're staying?"

I saw my mother turn her gaze from the mobile home to my Dad, who didn't miss a beat and said encouragingly, "Looks fine to me."

He got out of the car, opened up the hatchback and proceeded to bring luggage up to the door.

The three of us remained seated, as if unable to fully grasp the tin can that awaited our arrival. Finally Brian opened the door of the car and stepped outside. After scanning number seven's perimeters, he continued to look around and asked, "Where's the lake?"

"I guess it must be further down the road," my father said.

My mother and I got out of the car and walked dismally toward the entrance of the trailer. Heading up two steps, my father pulled back the half torn screen door, turned the key in the doorknob and opened it. We were hit by what felt like a blast of fire. The metal mobile home was a heat magnet, and inside it was absolutely stifling. Within seconds I realized there was no air conditioning. We spread out to open each and every window, hoping for a breeze. That's when Brian witnessed something traumatic.

"Dad!" he said running out from behind a door so narrow you had to press your arms against your body to get through. "I was opening the window in the bathroom when I looked out and saw another one of these trailers right next to us!"

"So what?" I declared.

"Well, I saw a person. It was a lady. A very fat lady. And she was..." My brother paused then shouted, "She was buck naked! It was awful, I didn't want to look but I couldn't help it!"

"Oh God," I said, glaring at my father. "I can't believe you made me come here. We can't even see the lake, and now this woman is walking around naked in another tin can that's practically on top of ours. And to think I could have been at Jess's pool party!"

"Relax," my father said quickly. "You haven't even given this place a chance yet. Now come help me get the canoe off the car."

By this time both my mother's and my hair began to frizz due to the heavy humidity, giving the impression we'd just been struck by lightning. This was turning into the trip from hell. Little did I know it would get worse.

* * *

I was in a full sweat by the time we unpacked all our stuff and took both the canoe and kayak off the roof.

My mother proposed we get in our bathing suits and head down to the lake for a swim. Her suggestion revived my spirits a bit, and I felt better just thinking about the cool water of a mountain lake.

My Dad insisted we bring both the canoe and the kayak with us. When no one volunteered to help him, he started dragging them himself. He quickly fell behind us, looking like an old pack mule that could drop dead in the heat at any moment. Out of guilt, Brian and I handed my mother our towels and drinks, and walked back to my Dad, where together we took the canoe from him. Using the two ropes tied to the canoe's bow, we pulled it along behind us, and it felt heavier than it looked. Although I couldn't tell for sure, I suspected Brian really wasn't pulling at all, but just faking it.

"Brian," I said, "I'm pulling all the weight, you've got to pull your share."

"I am!" he shouted back angrily.

It didn't matter. I could see the lake now, and it was just another 50 feet down to the right. Its blue water sparkled in the sun, and I couldn't wait to jump in.

We arrived at a sandy beach, where about twenty people were lying on lounge chairs, looking like toads roasting in the desert sun. It struck me as odd that no one was in the water. A lone lifeguard sat high up in a wooden chair atop a white platform.

Brian and I dropped the canoe ropes and sprinted down toward the lake, ready to dive in. But just as we reached the water's edge, the lifeguard blew his whistle. Alarmed, we stopped and turned around to see what the fuss was. He was shaking his head, pointing to a sign off to our left. We walked toward the sign that was bobbing on a float about five feet from shore and read it.

Beach Temporarily Closed.

What the heck? I thought. I walked over to the lifeguard, who looked younger than me, and even more miserable. His face was covered with oozing pimples; some so red it looked like he'd taken an electric sander to his face.

"Excuse me, why is the beach closed?" I asked.

The lifeguard shifted in his chair, and climbed down the three steps from his perch. I stepped back, not wanting to be too close, worried one of his larger pimples might jump off him and onto me. He beckoned me closer, and I warily took a half step toward him.

In a low voice he spoke into my ear, "We had to close the beach because some little kid pooped in the water."

I felt like he had just punched me in the stomach. "You've got to be kidding me," I stammered.

"I'm not kidding. It was pretty gross. That's the little kid over there," he said, jerking his head toward a family of five on a big red blanket. They sat beneath a huge beach umbrella that matched the blanket, and in the middle of the group was an open cooler. The father was drinking a Budweiser and the rest of the family looked like they were eating fried chicken, including a toddler who was naked.

"Jeeze," said Brian, standing behind me, "Is this place some kind of naked colony? First the fat lady and now this kid."

The lifeguard heard him. "You mean nudist colony," he said. "No, it's not, but as the lifeguard it's not my job to tell them how to dress. And I don't even know why they're eating, all the meals are free here when you rent a cabin."

I didn't want to ask him how he could call one of those tin cans a cabin, but I was curious about the free meals. "Is the food any good?"

"It's decent," he said.

Brian wasn't thinking about food. "So you mean we can't go in the water at all?"

"No," answered the lifeguard. "When this happens we have to shut the beach down for at least a couple hours."

"You mean it's happened before?" I blurted out.

"Oh yeah, it's been worse."

I didn't need to hear anymore and wheeled around, ready to head back toward the cabin. But my father, covered in sweat, had just arrived with the kayak dragging behind him. He paused, saw Brian and me standing there, and asked, "How come you're not in the water?"

"Because it's filled with poop!" Brian yelled.

"What are you talking about?"

"*Shhhhhh*," I said, taking a step toward my Dad. "See that float on the water with the sign? Well that's the poop float. It means we can't go swimming because some little kid decided to make this entire swimming section his toilet." I stole a glance at the family on the red blanket, all with their mouths open not to receive fried chicken now, but to stare at us in return.

My father looked absolutely crushed and stared right back at them.

With my already sour mood worsening, I stormed off in the direction of the trailers with Brian following after me like he was on a leash. Halfway back to the tin can, I whirled around and snapped at him. "Do you have to follow me everywhere?" I screamed.

"Well what else am I supposed to do?" he said. "I can't go in the water, and if I stay there Dad will want me to go out in the canoe. Besides, did you see what he was wearing?"

Unfortunately, I had noticed. He was wearing a bathing suit that was clearly one from his past. And by past, I mean from when he was sixteen years old. It was a faded greenish-gray, discolored and blotchy in the back. What was worse was its length, or lack thereof. The trunks were so short they looked like a pair of the hot-pants girls wore in the 1960's when mini-skirts and tie-dye was popular. And worst of all, he was shirtless. My father thought he was in tip-top shape because he did sit-ups. But the only difference the sit-ups made was that they pushed his belly up his torso a few inches. He was proud his gut didn't hang over his belt, but it looked like he was a few months pregnant, protruding outwards rather than hanging. In his mind his waist looked good, for he would continually say, "It's starting to look like a six-pack— I could pass for a thirty year old," only to find a blank face staring back.

But that *still* was not the worst part. Being a product of some odd medical procedure, my Dad does not have a belly button. No belly button like the rest of humankind. Just flat skin where there should be a hole.

I remember years ago when Brian first noticed our Dad had no belly button. The three of us were in our backyard playing in a tiny blue plastic pool on a hot summer day.

"Dad, what happened to your belly button? Where'd it go?" asked then-five-year-old Brian.

"It didn't go anywhere," my father said smiling fondly. "I've never had one."

"But doesn't everyone have a bellybutton?"

"Not me," he said in a proud manner.

"But why?"

"Well, I guess it's time you know the truth," he answered, shifting to a somber tone. "I was hatched."

At that point Brian looked my way, his eyes frantically searching me for a response that was to the contrary. But enjoying the story, I only nodded in enthusiastic agreement to the hatching claim. Horrified, Brian then bolted out of the pool and ran toward the house shouting, "Mom! Dad was hatched!"

The truth is my father's umbilical cord tore when he was born. "It was awful," he would say dramatically, as if he could remember the first day of his life. "The umbilical cord ripped out, leaving a giant hole in my stomach and guts were spilling out everywhere. The doctors had to push them back inside and stitch me up." With that image painted so vividly, Brian never brought up his missing belly button again.

But he didn't have to. Not long after Brian heard the belly button story we were at the beach and some kids standing by the water's edge near my father were gawking at his stomach. I was sitting on the beach blanket and couldn't hear what my father said, but it was clear he enjoyed the attention as he motioned the kids toward him and started talking.

When my father came back to the blanket I asked if he had told the kids the hatching story.

"No, of course not. I told them the truth. How I'd been attacked by a shark on this very beach and it bit exactly where my belly button was. I explained how I gave the shark a good punch in the snout which drove him off, but he swam away with the front part of my stomach in his mouth. You should have seen those kids' faces. They swallowed that story hook, line and sinker. I'll bet they don't even go in the water after this!"

* * *

And here I was a few years later, also avoiding the water, but for a different reason. I told Brian I wanted to be alone, and he went inside the tin can—probably to spy on the naked fat lady—while I continued walking. I went by a basketball court, a volleyball court, and even a little miniature golf course. Just beyond that was an open air pavilion with video games inside, and I wandered in. The room was empty except for two obnoxious ten-year-old boys, screaming as they played a virtual car driving game. Their yells and wild gesturing reminded me of the videos we watched in health class about people who overdosed on acid. Having given up on finding any place for solitude, I returned to the tin can to shower before dinner.

The bedroom Brian and I shared looked even smaller now than when I first set eyes on it. Brian had managed to throw his clothes all over the place so that it appeared a wild bear had just violently rummaged through his duffle bag. The room looked like a jail cell: it had one small window and a couple of mosquitoes buzzing around a lamp housed on a small wooden table in the corner. The two beds had bland blue comforters and were so close together that the passageway between them showed a mere sliver of the linoleum floor. With no fan and no AC, I was really looking forward to a cool shower.

With a towel wrapped around me, I left the cell and opened the two-foot wide bathroom door. I immediately pulled down the shade for fear of being seen, or worse, I might see the naked lady. Turning on the light, I looked the bathroom over. It was like being in a white, dimly lit porta-potty, equipped with a shower, toilet and sink. A nasty smell came from the toilet, which I suspected to be the work of Brian after following me back from the beach and into the cabin. With a grimace on my face, I closed the lid of the toilet and placed my towel on top of it. I then stepped inside the shower and closed the yellow curtain.

Being in this shower was like standing in a vertical coffin which encased its victim upright. I turned the knob and let cold water rush over me. Finally I was alone and at peace...

"Ahhhh!" The scream came from my mother in the kitchenette and was followed by the sound of shattered glass. I quickly turned off the water, threw on my towel and stepped outside sopping wet.

My Mom stood frozen by the kitchen sink, hands clutched at her chest, staring at the ground where shards of glass lay scattered across the tile floor.

"What happened?" I asked.

"I...I grabbed a glass from the cabinet to get a drink of water. When I filled it and held it up to my mouth," she said, making the motion with her hands of holding a glass of water to her face, "I...I saw a black spider swimming inside it! Ickkk!" she said reliving the moment again.

Great, I thought. *There are spiders in the cabinets, mosquitoes in the bedrooms. What's next, snakes in the bed sheets?*

After exiting the shower and catching a glimpse of my Mom sweeping up glass, I shut the door of my cell and pulled out jean shorts and an orange tank top from my bag and put them on. I combed my wet hair and threw it in a ponytail as my stomach rumbled a little, and I actually felt myself get a bit excited at the thought of dinner. Food always put me in a good mood, and I was curious to see what other teenagers there were around this place.

My father met Brian, my mother and myself outside of the trailer, wearing his infamous pink and turquoise striped shirt with green shorts, navy blue socks, and mud-stained sneakers. We walked along the dirt road towards the main office where we first entered the spider-infested trailer park. The sun was setting just over the horizon, creating a swirling mass of pink and orange across the summer night sky. During the walk we discussed how hungry we all were and how good a nice meal would be. It was the first time we found something to agree on.

As we turned right towards the main office and began following a path that wrapped behind it, there was a small basketball court in the distance with a sign off the trail that read:

Basketball Foul Shot Contest
Ages 8-12
Saturday 5pm
Shoot and Win!

"Look Brian," my father said pointing towards the sign. "There's something for you to do tomorrow. And I bet you'll be good at it." Brian gave a grunt and nodded. He had been playing for years in our town's recreational basketball league, so this contest would be a good challenge for him.

We approached a white rectangular building overlooking the lake, with many windows and two large glass double doors in the front. As I opened the doors and stepped onto the wood floor, a rush of refreshing cool air hit my face and I gave a loud exhale.

Ahh. Air conditioning, finally.

Off to the right we found a table draped in a maroon tablecloth with a white folded card in its center labeled **Tougias.** In the middle of the hardwood dining room was a very long table with many lights reflecting onto metal trays. We headed towards the far end, Brian grabbing a large white plate before anyone else could, and started in a train-like fashion down the buffet.

The first silver tray housed what appeared to be iceberg lettuce mixed carelessly with carrots and cucumbers, plastered in some sort of clear dressing. Brian moved forward without so much as even a glance at the salad, and I too took a pass, thinking it looked more like soup than salad. Next in line were slices of white bread, one flopping over the next as though they had wilted and died. I continued on to what looked like a sea of green pebbles, many of them mashed together and flattened around the tray's edges. They were peas that looked like they had been sitting out for days in the heat, only to be thrown in some butter and served for dinner. Next was corn on the cob. I thought, *how do you mess up corn?* Luckily, there were no visible flaws in the tray of yellow corn, and I picked two up and placed them onto my plate.

I paused before moving forward to find out how the rest of the family was making out. Brian had already reached the end of the buffet, looking confused as his eyes searched desperately up and down the table, as if about to say, *where's the rest?* To my left were my parents. My mother was holding a pea up to the light, inspecting it as though she had found a rare gem, while my father was still back at the first tray, carefully scooping out the salad so the dressing wouldn't splash all over. I noticed he had a little system. He would lift a small scoop of lettuce up above the giant salad bowl and let the dressing cascade back into it before placing it on his plate. He looked quite satisfied with his little technique, but he was holding up the growing line of people behind him, who looked ready to dunk his head in the bowl.

Further down the table of wonders I traveled, only to find another tray with what appeared to be clam chowder, but tinged with a yellowish hue. I ruled that option out fairly quickly, and I found myself in front of North Lake's feature entrée. The only word I can use to describe the contents in the metal tray staring back at me is glop. *What is that? That cannot be edible...*

I concluded that the mound of chunky orange glop was someone's disastrous attempt at macaroni and cheese. I stood staring at it, not believing that I had come to the end of the line. *This was what we had come here for? This was what I had missed the big pool party for?*

With nothing but corn on my plate, I made my way back to the table. As I took my seat, I looked around at the other families that had gathered in the dining hall. There was a husband and wife with their two young daughters, staring blankly down at their plates, the girls dissecting their food with their forks. Off to the right was the family from the beach. I looked at the child who was responsible for shutting down the beach, his hands and face covered in the orange mess that was macaroni and cheese. I thought, *No wonder—probably couldn't control himself after eating this food.* On the other side of them was an older, well-dressed couple, eating slowly and cautiously. But there were other families who seemed to be eating, laughing and talking, and I wondered if they'd also been drinking.

After finishing the ears of corn, Brian and I went back up to the serving area, this time to the dessert table to stock up on chocolate chip cookies for fear breakfast might be a pea-and-macaroni omelet. By the time we got back to the tin can it was 8:45 p.m. Exhausted and sweating inside the metal shell, I flung myself on my bed. I wondered what was happening at Jess's pool party and prayed tomorrow would be better than today.

* * *

I awoke the next day from a nightmare that I went to the pool party, removed my cover-up and was met by 20 scrutinizing sets of eyes belonging to my peers, who one by one began pointing at me and laughing hysterically. When I looked down, I realized my bathing suit was coated in a gooey orange glop substance. Mortified, I immediately jumped in the pool to remove the glop. When I surfaced, I was only met by more cackling and pointing from the many guys and girls, all keeled over holding their stomachs as their laughter intensified. Confused, I whipped my head around and saw next to me a brown floater just like the one at North Lake.

After waking up in a sweaty panic and discovering the various bug bites on my body, I ate a granola bar and a banana for breakfast and went back into my room to change for the beach. It was incredibly difficult to get from one room to the next in the tiny trailer. We were constantly bumping into one another, like four over-sized fish stuck in a minute rectangular aquarium of tepid water.

I stayed at the beach most of the day, which thankfully re-opened for swimming. I wondered what was happening back home, how many big things I was already missing, if anyone had even noticed that *I* was missing. I dreamt about the Internet and my air conditioned room. I pictured hot fudge sundaes and French fries—anything that would get me through the day and take my mind off this place.

For lunch there were sandwiches and chips at the North Lake Resort dining hall. They weren't gourmet, but they looked consumable. I had two late in the afternoon because I decided it would be best to skip dinner, and of course Brian did the same. My parents were invited to a lobster dinner with the resort's owners, so Brian and I would be left back at the trailer for a few hours.

"Hey Kristin," my father bellowed when I re-entered the tin can. "I just met a woman who is also a travel writer here, and she has two girls around your age. I told her to have them stop by before we left for the lobster dinner, so you would have someone to hang out with while Brian plays in his basketball tournament."

"Oh. Ah...thanks Dad," I said shakily.

I was not in the mood for an awkward forced encounter with two teenage girls. But I figured, *if their mom is a travel writer they're likely feeling stuck in this miserable place the same as me, and we'll have plenty to talk about.*

After a shower, I picked out a pair of jean shorts and a lime green halter-top from my bag and put my hair into two braids. The family wished Brian luck as he set off to the basketball court for his contest.

Shortly after he left there was a knock at the trailer door. My father opened it with my mother standing behind him.

"Hi Cindy, how are you?"

"Good, thanks!" replied a tall woman with a large build and

short, puffy blonde hair. She said hello to my mother, then looking at me she said, "Hello, you must be Kristin! My daughters Stacey and Patty are just outside the door sitting on a picnic bench."

As Cindy and my parents headed off for drinks and their lobster dinner, I too left the comfort of the tin can and began walking around its side toward a picnic bench.

As I turned the corner to meet the girls, I was immediately taken back by what sat before me. A girl with a mass of purple hair was staring at me. The other sister was facing the opposite direction but her head was just as bright. Neon green highlights were streaked through her brown hair, and she was chewing absentmindedly on several strands of it. After saying hello and introducing myself, the purple haired girl said in a monotone voice, "I'm Stacey. This is my sister Patty," gesturing toward the underwhelmed girl sitting across from her.

"Hi," Patty said insipidly, barely making an effort to turn around. I walked over and sat next to her. She looked at me and said, "Got any cigs?"

I stared at the green eyebrow piercing she had just above her left eye. "Uh ... no," I stammered, "Are you enjoying your trip here?"

"Hell no," she shot back, accusingly. "We got no cigs, the food sucks, and there's nothing to do."

"Yea, the food sure does suck," I said, trying to sound tough. Then she got right to the heart of the matter. "So, you do any drugs?"

Never having so much as made eye contact with a drug, my heart began to pound. I tried not to act too surprised and said, "no." But when that was met with disapproving glares, I tried a more neutral response, casually saying, "Not lately."

For the first time Patty looked at me, started to say something, and then apparently changed her mind.

So these were the regulars who stayed at North Lake, I thought to myself. Here I was, finally with girls my own age, and the only topic of conversation had revolved around cigarettes and illegal drugs. Stacey started talking about her top five places to hide marijuana, while I nodded, looking at her purple hair, wondering how often she colored it. I felt like I was listening to someone whose brain had been deep-fried at McDonald's then thrown back into his or her head. Worse, I was trapped at this picnic bench with Patty and Stacey, and no one was around to rescue me. I thought of how my health teacher was always saying, *"Don't do drugs, kids. There's chemicals in them that will rot your brains out."* I wondered if that teacher had somehow met Stacy and Patty.

I heard our trailer's screen door slam, and I knew Brian had returned. I stood up and said, "Well, I should really go see how my brother did at basketball. It was nice meeting you both!"

As I began to walk away, Patty called out, "If you find any cigs, let us know!"

And with that I quickly returned to the trailer. Brian was sitting on his bed, restlessly unlacing his sneakers.

"How'd it go?" I asked.

"I got second place," he said, holding up a small blue ribbon.

"Well that's great!"

He didn't look at me, but struggled to untie a knot in the laces of one of his sneakers, before giving up and yanking the sneaker off and flinging it toward his duffel bag.

"If you got second place, why are you so mad?" I asked gently.

"Because I was the only one there!" he said.

"I don't understand?"

"When I showed up for the foul shot contest," he grunted, pulling his other sneaker off his foot, "I was the only one there. After the two teenage boys running the contest realized no one else was coming, they handed me the basketball and I stepped up to the foul line. I needed to make three foul shots in a row to win."

"So you only made two?"

"No!" Brian yelled. "I made all three right in a row, and they gave me second place. It doesn't make any sense!"

"This *place* doesn't make any sense," I said, laughing at the absurdity of the trip for the first time.

But the vacation hadn't even reached the height of its misery.

* * *

My parents returned around 9 p.m. I was bored as ever, so my father asked if Brian and I wanted to take a walk.

"Bring that big can of bug spray when you come out," he said.

I put on my sneakers, grabbed the super-sized can of repellant and stepped outside the trailer to spray myself. There was only a sliver of light made by the moon reflecting off the side of the trailer's metal.

My father was standing about ten feet away in the dark, his silhouette barely visible against the backdrop of the black trees. After I had sprayed my body I called to my father and in one swift motion tossed the heavy can his way.

He didn't see it coming.

It slammed him square in the head and he let out a wail trailed by an echo that reverberated off every trailer in the vicinity.

This was followed by a terrible, tense silence. *Oh crap.* My eyes widened and my heart started pounding. I couldn't believe how stupid I had just been. I had *definitely* become dumber after my encounter with the cigarette girls.

In the dim light I could see my father holding one hand to his forehead and taking a step toward me as he roared, "What the hell did you do that for!"

My always even-tempered Dad was mad. Very mad. I didn't have to see his face to know he was fuming—I could sense the fury in his voice. I immediately whirled around and ran back into the tin can faster than I've ever run in my life. I jumped on my mother's bed where she was lying watching TV, and I yelled hysterically as wet tears rolled down my face, "DAD'S GOING TO KILL ME!"

I could hear my father in the kitchen muttering. My mother hopped out of bed, and I heard her say, "Let me get some ice on that cut." She opened the freezer and cracked some ice out of the ice cube tray. Then she said, "What happened out there?"

This was my cue to move into my own room, close the door and crawl into bed. Through the paper thin wall I listened to my father say, "It was Kristin. I don't know what she was thinking but without warning she hurled the bug spray at me. And now look at me, it looks like I've been in a bar fight. Tomorrow people will ask what happened. And I'll just say, 'Oh my daughter was just showing her appreciation for this vacation... and hit me with a can of Off!!'"

* * *

We packed up early the next morning and during the car ride back to Massachusetts no one spoke more than a few words. I sat silent, not daring to complain to my father about the blue cooler jutting into my ribs. No one knew what to say after that trip to North Lake. But there was one thing that certainly didn't need to be said: we were never going back.

* * *

A Dad's View

I was like a fish chasing after the lure of a free trip, and figured how could we go wrong with an all expenses paid mini vacation? Granted, the excursion didn't go entirely as planned, but the family was together and that's what's important. Kristin may not agree with that sentiment, and she has pointed out that I should have researched North Lake Resort before I made the decision to go. But there were simply some aspects of the trip that no one could have anticipated, such as the kid pooping in the lake and the 100 degree heat. Had either of those things not happened, the trip could have been a rousing success. Kristin met some girls her own age that she might have stayed in touch with, and Brian placed a strong second in the big basketball shootout. (I'll bet he would have gotten first place if he hadn't been distracted by seeing the nude woman the day before. I'm not even sure there was a naked lady in the trailer next to ours because I checked a couple times and saw nothing. Maybe the little tyke was dreaming—after all, he was getting to that age.)

The trailer was a tad stuffy, I admit, but the lobster dinner my wife and I had was first class. I'm not sure why the kids complained incessantly about the food.

At times I was more than a little perturbed—not at the resort, mind you, but at my own two kids who whined about things you would expect to find up in New Hampshire, such as the black spiders and the mosquitoes. At least I kept my sense of humor, and asked Kristin if she'd "like a little cheese with her whine." Having a sense of humor when others are down in the dumps shows good fatherly leadership qualities: a Dad has to stay loose at all times. Although, truth be told, I did briefly lose my composure when the industrial size can of bug spray hit me in the head.

So while the trip wasn't the greatest, everyone got out of the house for the weekend, saw some new things, and spent time together. And I made a point to tell Kristin that Jess's pool party was no big deal, and that "you only have one father."

With Kristin entering high school, I expected she would continue maturing and soon see the wisdom of spending more time with Dear Old Dad. Or so I hoped. Either way, it was going to be an interesting year.

CHAPTER 2

THE FIRST DAY IS THE WORST DAY

Summer left as quickly as it came. Of course I had missed the social highlight of the entire season, that being Jess's pool party, but I did manage to salvage some of my social status by going on a date (my first date to be precise). His name was Sean, and we had been going to school together since third grade.

Me, Sean, his twin Tom and my friend Alyssa decided to go on a double date to the movies. Of course Alyssa and I spent hours in my room, changing outfits and doing each other's makeup. The whole time I was wondering if Sean and I would hold hands or kiss during the movie. I knew I liked him and I was so happy he asked me out.

My mother decided to take Brian to a movie also, so she conveniently drove us to the theater where we met the boys. The four of us sat down in the front row. "I'll be right back," Sean said, turning to me as he got up from his seat. He came back a few minutes later, with popcorn and a perplexed look on his face.

"Kristin," he said.

"Yea?" I replied smiling expectantly, imaging that what came next was him telling me how happy he was to be at the movies with me or something equally endearing.

"Isn't that your Mom?" he asked, looking behind us.

My stomach dropped into what felt like a bottomless pit as I turned my gaze away from him, looking back into the faces of the audience. I spotted Brian and my mother sitting just four rows behind us. *Nooooooo!* I wanted to scream. They were both staring at me—my brother with a slight grin. Light from the movie screen danced across his face in a frenzy, similar to the way my emotions swirled with resentment. I knew they were coming to see a movie, but I didn't realize it was going to be the *same* movie.

I couldn't utter a word the entire time. Sean looked equally uncomfortable, and certainly weirded out. Still, he asked me a couple questions during the movie and I just nodded like the village idiot. I was too flustered and self-conscious having my mother and Brian directly behind me, watching my every move. The worst part is that I actually liked Sean, and really hoped he liked me, but when the movie was over all I could muster was a quick "thanks" and not a word more, my embarrassment paralyzing me. *Would all my dates be as bad as this? Would I ever even go on another date?* Other girls my age had steady boyfriends, and I had just blown my first date. Needless to say it didn't work out with Sean.

* * *

Freshman Orientation was a blur. The inside of my high school, with its endless tunnel-like hallways, seemed incredibly confusing and complex. Luckily I was with most of my friends, and we arrived with our mothers all in a chatter about how they could not believe we were going to be in high school. At that point we received a small slip of paper from the orientation leader, a junior named Jared Halpert with perfectly aligned teeth and a blazing white smile. No one was able to utter a word in front of him since we were too busy gawking at his massive biceps. On the slip of paper was the location and combination of the lockers we were assigned. *C-74* mine read. Not having any idea where that was, I looked to my friends for some assurance. Surely we would be put together seeing as how we were all freshman.

"What'd you guys get?" I asked.

"Mine says F-26," Laura said without lifting her eyes from the slip of paper.

"I have my locker in F Wing too!" shrieked Jess excitedly.

I frantically looked to Michelle, who had not yet answered.

"D-16," she said blankly.

"Alright everyone, now go find your lockers and try out the combinations. I'll be walking around if anyone needs any help," Jared yelled over the murmur of excited teenage voices.

With my map of the high school in hand, my mother and I left the main entrance and ventured off to scout out my locker. *Please be somewhere central,* I muttered to myself. We began to walk down the main hall, which I soon realized was F Wing after seeing Laura and Jess squeal when they found their lockers nearly side by side. Main hall was a prime social location. It was a long corridor in which all other halls branched off of. Further down its gray speckled tile we walked, passing D Wing where Michelle was hurriedly jiggling her lock. We kept going, and at this point there were no other freshman with their parents walking in front of us. I looked behind me and saw a boy who looked like he was in fifth grade still searching for his locker with his worried mother. Behind them in the distance were scattered freshman, opening and closing their lockers and looking to see who had lockers around them.

Finally after what felt like a mile long walk, I saw the blue sign labeled "C-Wing" to my left. We turned and entered the dimly lit hallway, my mother and I searching for the number 74. It was not until passing six classrooms that I found my locker. The only other freshman located in C-Wing in that orientation group was the boy who looked like a fifth grader. I tried the combination as my mother watched over my shoulder. It opened with ease, and I looked inside its blue shiny interior. It was about as tall as me— five feet four inches, with two hooks at the top.

"Well this isn't too bad," my mother commented with forced cheerfulness, her voice resonating though the cavernous hall. I closed and secured the locker and left without saying a word. This would be my territory throughout my whole freshman year. It would be where I spent the majority of my time. Yet here I was off in the boonies with Fifth Grade Francis to keep me company. Even when she said, "this isn't too bad," I knew deep down my mother felt my dismay.

The remainder of our orientation was spent touring the school. I had knots in my stomach just thinking of my first day. What would I wear? Would I remember how to get to my homeroom? Who else would I have a locker next to? The dread hit me like a hundred foot wave. I had only three days to sort out my apprehensive thoughts.

The night before the first day of school I was online chatting with my friends. I had assumed everybody was taking the bus to school, so I asked Laura what bus she was on.

"Bus!" she typed in response. "No way would I be caught dead going to high school on the BUS! LOL. Jennifer Dwyer is driving me to school."

Jennifer Dwyer was a senior who we knew from dance. Of course Laura had already arranged to step into school with a popular upperclassman, how silly of me to think she would take the bus with us common folk. When I asked Jess the same question, she said her mom would be driving her to school. My twin friends Michelle and Dara had their older brother to drive them to school, and I had no one. Now I was no longer just nervous about school, I was also nervous about getting there. Yet I decided not to say anything to my parents for fear my father would volunteer to drive me the first day—in *that* car.

* * *

The sound of the alarm broke my fitful sleep. It was 6:25am, and I felt like my head had been slammed by a brick. Incredibly groggy, I forced my comatose body out of bed and into the shower. I brushed my teeth, put on the outfit I had laid out the night before, and scrunched my wet hair with two palms full of anti-frizz mousse. My green L.L. Bean backpack displaying the embroidered initials "KAT" was packed with heavy textbooks, and I threw it over my shoulders after kissing my mother goodbye.

"Wait!" she yelled, as the garage door was about to shut. "You forgot your lunch!" I ran back in and grabbed the brown paper bag. "Bye Mom!" I said, winded.

Walking down the driveway and turning onto the street, I heard my mother yell again. She was running after me in her bathrobe and pink fuzzy slippers. I glanced quickly around, hoping no other kids were within sight. "You didn't eat breakfast!" My mother croaked when she reached me. In one hand was an apple and in the other a blueberry muffin.

"I don't have time to eat, Mom," I said brusquely.

"Ok, ok, then I'll just put this apple in your backpack, and you can eat it on the bus."

"Not if I miss it!" I blurted, rolling my eyes as she unzipped a side pocket and slid in the apple.

God, I hope no one is watching.

"Good luck!" she said turning back toward our house.

Without looking back I waved my arm and walked as fast as I could toward the bus stop, which was located just over a half a mile down the street from the house.

Waiting there were three other kids with familiar faces— all upperclassmen I recognized from middle school, none of whom I spoke to. I was anxious to see who else would be on the bus. Three awkward minutes of silence passed until I finally heard a rumbling sound, and the yellow school bus rounded the corner. I was the last to get on, and after walking up the steps and looking around, I saw that the bus was empty. *We must be the first stop,* I thought to myself. I sat somewhere in the middle as the driver hit the gas. He was an older man, with white hair and a large gut. Looking at his left hand on the wheel, I noticed that he had no thumb, and wondered if he could grip the wheel hard enough to really steer. I hoped so, because he drove that bus like a racecar.

Ten minutes passed, and still no sign of a recognizable companion. Finally, I saw my friend Alyssa outside the window as we rode downhill to meet another group of teenagers anxiously waiting. When she got on the bus I waved to her, and with a smile she waved back but took a quick turn and sat with a boy a few seats in front of me. *How does she know him?* I wondered as they talked. I knew he was in our grade, but I couldn't think of his name or why Alyssa sat with him and not me.

The ride to school was a half an hour long and I ended up sitting with a boy whose backpack took up a good portion of the seat. I pressed my forehead miserably against the dirty window as the bus turned into the entrance of the high school. Looking out into the student parking lot, I saw Laura getting out of Jennifer's car, her bag on one arm and a Dunkin' Donuts coffee in the other. I was analyzing her outfit when all of a sudden my body flew upwards and my forehead hit the glass as my butt came back down to smack the surface of the cracked leather seat. *Ouch,* I muttered while rubbing my now pulsing forehead with my fingers. We had just driven over a speed bump and the driver made no attempt to slow down.

I kept my hand to my head and rubbed the spot that had slammed into the glass window, and I could feel the bruise rising as the seconds passed. *As if I'm not already the total image of some uncool freshman reject who rides the bus, now I have a red bump on my forehead to complete the look.*

The bus came to a halt in the front of the school, and I felt my stomach do flips as I watched the mass of animated students ambling in through the double doors. I stepped out of the bus and began to walk in step with the herd of students, all dressed to make a favorable impression on the first day of school. We approached the main entrance where the sound of excited voices flooded the air. My mouth felt terribly dry.

I turned right to walk down main hall towards my locker in C-Wing. Making my way through the corridor I couldn't help but look from side to side. There were girls hugging, decorating lockers and brushing their hair. Huge guys were grabbing notebooks and Gatorades. To my right was a group of kids playing some sort of card game on the floor while simultaneously eating bagels. There was commotion everywhere; people reuniting and catching up on their summers, pens and calculators flying in and out of lockers, a large white milk spill already on the floor that everyone was cautiously avoiding, girls adjusting their outfits and applying lip gloss.

When I entered C Wing it did not feel like it did before. Rather than being empty and quiet, it resounded with the noise of busy students plopping notebooks inside the metal lockers and slamming the doors before scouting out friends or classrooms. I had a difficult time wedging my way into the tiny space in front of my locker since two kids were already occupying the ones next to me.

"Kristin!" someone shouted directly next to me. It was Katie Long, my childhood friend dating back to age three. We had lost touch over the years after we both moved out of our old neighborhood and were sent to different middle schools.

"Oh my God, Katie!" I replied, opening my arms to hug her. "How weird is this that after growing up together, our freshman year we have lockers right next to one another?"

"I know!" she said excitedly. "So we must have the same homeroom then, because our lockers are where our first period classes are."

"Do you have mister ..." I glanced down at my schedule. "Mr. Tetlan for geometry?"

"Yes!" she shouted.

I was now a little more at ease knowing Katie was in my class and had a locker next to mine.

"What happened to your forehead?" Katie asked, narrowing her eyes and taking a step toward me.

"Oh it's nothing. Our crazy bus driver almost gave me a concussion." As soon as the words left my mouth I knew they were a mistake.

"You took the bus?"

"Yeah, and please keep this between you and me. Hopefully

nobody else will know."

Katie nodded gravely, lips pursed, as if I had just confided in her that I had leprosy. I changed the subject and asked about her summer and family before finally heading into the classroom.

The first day of school gives no indication of what classes will really be like. All day the teachers talked, and we listened. They introduced themselves, the course, and what we would be learning over the next year. At about 11 o'clock the bell rang as it had many times already, but a new wave of trepidation hit me as I realized this bell was summoning us into the cafeteria. Who could I find to sit with?

Jammed with buzzing hungry students, I stood by the door of the lunchroom for a while surveying the congested scene, my bagged lunch clenched tightly in my hand. The large cafeteria was swarming with people flocking to round tables containing about ten seats each, and I didn't recognize a soul in my lunch period. There appeared to be a hundred round tables accompanied by open mouths that were either talking or chewing.

I felt overwhelmed by the commotion, my eyes frantically scanning the faces, desperately hoping for a friendly gesture or wave of a nearby friend. I recognized no one. The thought of walking to the other side of the cafeteria where people might see me looking like a lost puppy was daunting. But it was better than standing there, feeling like I'd break into tears. I took a deep breath, set off through the chaos and quickly scooted over to a table that still had a couple empty seats. There was a shaggy haired boy with what looked like a beginner's mustache eating a slice of pepperoni pizza and a small girl munching on a turkey sandwich. Next to her was another girl with glasses, whose frizzy hair framed her face like a perfect triangle.

"Hello," I said. "Are you all freshmen too?"

They nodded, and we grunted a few words back and forth. But mainly they just stared at me in between bites. From my brown paper bag I pulled out my juice box, turkey sandwich and Goldfish crackers.

I was eating in silence when all of a sudden I heard, "Kristin!" accompanied by some laugher. I whirled around to see Laura and Dara giggling as they approached me. "We just noticed you and came to rescue you, we're sitting right over there," they said laughing and pointing to a table with some boys off in the distance. I felt immediately relieved and jammed my food back into the paper bag. But a sense of guilt also surged through me as the three students I'd been sitting with watched me rise and leave the table in a flash.

At the new table, the topic of conversation for the next fifteen minutes was just what I thought it would be. How I looked like a lost soul, sitting by my lonesome self on what they said was the "loser side" of the cafeteria. Rather than express my irritation I let them laugh it off. Of course they noticed the bump on my forehead. One of the boys at the table looked up from his sandwich and muttered, "You look like a Cyclops."

Laughter broke out, and I thought, *I have to come up with an explanation that doesn't involve the bus.*

"I had a wicked wipe out waterskiing two days ago and the ski hit my head. I'm still learning to slalom." I could barely ski on two skis, but this total fabrication seemed to work, and they let the Cyclops comment pass. It was a close call, as I knew a nasty nickname can stay with you for all of high school.

The rest of the day was a drag. On the bus ride home I looked over my assignment notebook, in which I had noted some math problems, a chapter in my biology book to read, and a reminder to bring gym clothes to avoid receiving a zero for the day.

Back at home the smell of something freshly baked met me as I dropped my backpack in the kitchen. A plate of chocolate chip cookies was awaiting me on the stove, accompanied by my mother reading a magazine at the kitchen table.

"Kwiti!" she said in a high-pitched voice, smiling as she stood up to greet me. Kwiti is an alteration of Kristi, a nickname only my mother calls me.

"Hi Mom," I said as she came to hug me.

My Mom stood back a minute after the hug.

"What happened to your head?"

"I really don't want to talk about it. But I'm fine."

My Mom started to say something, then paused, and said, "So tell me all about your first day of high school!"

"Well...there's really not much to tell," I said, shrugging my shoulders as I wrangled myself out of her arms and across the kitchen to snag a cookie. "My classes seem fine. I don't have too many friends in them though. The cafeteria is huge...and that's really it. I'm going to go change for dance." I headed upstairs and into my room to avoid further questioning.

I had been a competitive dancer for nearly ten years at a dance studio located in my town. Dance didn't really bring me the same joy it once had, but I couldn't quite break away since it was such a big part of my life outside of school.

I put on a black leotard and red shorts. I opened my purple dance bag, which was steadily falling apart since it had been a sewing project for my seventh grade life skills class. Those were some real "life-skills"—how to make a flimsy gym bag. I checked to make sure my jazz, ballet, pointe, and tap shoes were all inside.

My mother dropped me off at the studio, where my friends were already sitting in a close huddle, undoubtedly discussing their first day.

"Hey guys," I said making my way over to where they were conversing. They all said hello, and I couldn't help but notice how vibrant and chipper they all looked.

"I love my classes!" Laura exclaimed to the rest of the huddle. "Josh Matthews is in my math class, and Lance Hurst is in my gym and health! We played this math game, and me and Josh were partners and he was just like, so funny!"

For fifteen minutes I sat there, listening to the various thrills each girl experienced on their first day. Why did I have no exciting news? Perhaps it was because most of my friends primarily took standard classes while I was in honors, where the hot guys were nowhere to be found. I realized that was why I had so few people I knew in my classes—apparently all the "cool people" took the "cool courses".

My dance instructor ordered everybody to the middle of the floor, where we began choreography for our company's jazz routine. None of us even had time to stretch because we were all so feverishly chatting with one another about school. With every new dance we learned, I was slowly being moved further and further in the back rows. Last year I was in the front of nearly all the dances, but at this rate I would soon be pushed into the wings of the stage where no on could see me. Luckily, twins Dara and Michelle were back there with me. We were the only girls who did another sport aside from dance, which was softball in the spring. Thus, we missed more classes than everyone else, and I suppose this was our punishment.

Dance was stressful that afternoon, and three hours later I

couldn't wait to go home. Before we left, my friend Molly was asked by our dance instructor to try on a pair of black jazz pants, which would be part of her solo costume. She was an incredibly skinny girl, with long thin legs that looked like pipe cleaners. When Molly complained that they were far too small and tight, the instructor said "nonsense" and took the pants from her. She then put them on her own 40-something-year-old body, and my friends and I stopped zipping our bags to gape in astonishment. Over the course of a year, this woman had managed to turn into a workout fanatic and dropped 30 pounds to "get her bod back." She didn't waste a second showing off her new figure in skin-tight outfits, which was still quite shapely. And she would bring up her miraculous weight loss to anyone who would listen.

"Look!" she said to Molly while kicking her legs to her face like a Rockette in the snug black spandex pants. There were pink rhinestones all over them that sparkled and glimmered with the slightest movement. "These fit me, and they'll fit you!" she barked.

I had to bite my bottom lip to keep from bursting into laughter, and I knew every other person in that room was struggling to do the same. You could see every single crack and crevice in her lower body, and it wasn't pretty. Under her breath, Jess muttered, "If she farts, all those rhinestones are going to fly off."

I snorted and placed my hand over my mouth. Uncontrollably giggling, my friends and I headed into the lobby.

"Oh jeeze, look," Laura said, and we all turned around to see what she was talking about.

Taped to the wall were pictures of dance girls from competitions, and all of the photos had one thing in common. They were taken by Mrs. Welch (the studio's unofficial photographer), which meant each photo had her daughter in it somewhere. Ginny Welch was what we like to call a "rising star" at the dance studio. She was about seven years old and was quickly moving up through the ranks and already had her own solo. Her mother couldn't get enough of the limelight for Ginny and had a hard time acknowledging the existence of any girl who wasn't her daughter. But that was the trend among most Moms at the dance studio—the place was a breeding ground for obnoxious stage moms.

All the photos had Ginny Welch somewhere in them, even if it was just her ponytail. We were searching for pictures that had us in them and plucked them off the wall.

"Here Dara, I found one of me and you," Michelle said while removing the photo from the blue wall. We all gathered around to look at it. Michelle turned the picture over, where the words *Michelle and Dara (Ginny, upper-right)* were written. It was the two of them on stage, and you could just barely make out the outline of half of Ginny's body in the shadows of the background. We all laughed, rolled our eyes and went home.

My Dad was watching CNN news—doing his usual muttering about politics— when I walked into the family room.

He brightened up when he saw me and turned the TV off. "Kristin, tell me all about your first day!"

"Eh, it was okay I guess."

Then I told him about Mom running down the street in her bathrobe, smacking my head on the bus window, sitting with strangers before my friends found me, and then putting up with their teasing.

"I know what you mean," my Dad said, surprising me, "I've been there."

"What do you mean?"

"Have I ever told you how I lost the championship wrestling match because of diarrhea?"

I wasn't sure how this related or if I wanted to hear about it. "You mean you got diarrhea during the match?" I asked, horrified at what he might say next.

"No, no, nothing that bad, but bad enough."

He then explained that his eighth grade gym coach arranged a wrestling tournament in four weight classes that every boy in the school had to participate in. My Dad had won all his preliminary matches to meet his archrival, Fred Turgent, in the finals for the lightweight division. The finals were to be held during a special assembly where the entire student body was required to attend. Apparently everyone in school was talking about the showdown, and kids were even betting on who would win.

"Well," he continued, "I truly thought I could beat him. One of the kids I beat in the semi-finals had wrestled both of us, and he thought I was the tougher opponent. I could almost see my name on the trophy. Then two days before the match my father did something he'd never done before. He took me out to dinner. Just me and him. I think after all the trouble I had caused him by being a wild kid, he was glad I had finally done something positive and reached the finals of the wrestling tournament. He took me to the Tuk-Puk-La Chinese restaurant. It was wonderful. My father even had two martinis, and joked and laughed as if he were a friend rather than my father."

My Dad paused here, shaking his head as a sad smile spread across his face. For a moment I thought he was choked up remembering the moment. But then he gritted his teeth and looked up. "After that dinner came the worst two days of my life."

"What happened?"

"That night I went home, went to bed, and woke up a few hours later feeling awful. I tossed and turned all night, feeling like I was getting the flu. In the morning I had shooting pains through my stomach and couldn't go to school. By noon I had the worst case of diarrhea of my life. I was praying it would go as quickly as it came, because the next day was the big match with Fred Turgent."

He went on to explain that things only got worse. His illness continued, and that evening the phone started ringing. Friends of my Dad were calling up to talk with him, asking him why he wasn't in school that day.

"What's worse is that two of my friends started telling people I was faking being sick just to avoid wrestling Fred Turgent. I felt betrayed, but beyond that I felt weaker by the hour. The next morning the diarrhea was gone and it took all my energy with it. I was so wiped out, I knew I couldn't compete in the match with any real strength, and stayed home from school. When I returned a day later, you can imagine what the kids were saying."

This might have been the first time in my life I felt sad for my father. Up until now, he just always seemed so steady, so determined, that I felt his life must have always been full of success and positivity. It was comforting to know that at my age, he was as vulnerable as me.

"Kristin," he said, "I've always kicked myself for not going to that match and giving it my best try. Anything would have been better than kids saying I was scared. And who knows, maybe I was. The thing is, that happened more than 30 years ago, and I remember it like it was yesterday. So many of the things that happened to me when I was a teenager still seem so....so raw, so poignant. I don't know if it's just me or if everyone has such feelings about the big events in their teenage years. But I guess what I'm saying is if you always do your best, you will never have any regrets, and the things other people say won't matter so much."

I wasn't sure what to say. This was a different side of my goofy, eccentric and fun-loving father.

"Thanks, Dad. You made me feel better. And thank god I've never had anything *that* embarrassing happen to me."

Had our conversation ended there, I would have left like I could handle whatever high school threw at me. But my Dad wasn't done.

"Well, actually you had your own little episode of poor judgment which caused quite a sensation, and was embarrassing for both of us!"

"What?"

"You probably don't even remember it, because you were just six years old. But I'll never forget it, and I doubt the neighbors will either."

"You're not going to bring up the ..."

My Dad cut me off, and said, "Yes, the *Flower Incident.*"

"Oh God, that was soooo long ago...."

The Flower Incident was something I had tried to forget, and had done so successfully, until this very moment. It was spring, and I must have been in about first grade. My friend Samantha was visiting and we took a walk through our neighborhood, looking for something to do. First we explored some woods and discovered a stone foundation of an old house and pretended we lived there. When that got boring we walked to the end of our street and on the way started picking flowers.

The first flowers we picked were by the side of the road, and the next ones were on one of those islands of shrubbery and woodchips people have landscaped into their yards. I guess we got carried away, because soon we were picking flowers that grew along neighbor's walkways and even in flowerpots. We accumulated a colorful array of daisies, tulips, roses, and other species I couldn't name, and started to take the entire pile home. We should have kept walking home but instead got an idea which seemed brilliant at the time.

My Dad interrupted the uncomfortable memory. "I remember that day very clearly. You and Samantha not only picked every flower in the neighborhood, you then tried to sell them back to the people whose yard you picked them from! Mrs. Scott called the house and said, *'Do you know what your daughter is doing? Well, she and her friend picked every one of the flowers I worked so hard to grow. Some of these flowers are quite expensive and even rare. I'm not sure what kind of children you're raising.'* That last comment got me mad, but I bit my tongue and then slowly said, 'I'm very sorry. If you want I'll reimburse you for the flowers. My daughter's a good kid and I will talk to her.' Then Mrs. Scott kind of shouted into the phone at me, *'You don't understand. After she and her friend picked the flowers, they knocked on my door and said they had flowers for sale and that it would only cost me five dollars! Those were my own flowers!'"*

I was mortified hearing this story again. It was the most immoral thing I'd ever done. "Dad, don't remind me, don't say anymore."

"Well," my father said, "I only bring it up to point out that you've had bad days using poor judgment before, and you'll have bad days again. But you'll always bounce back, because you learn from your mistakes quickly and possess inner strength."

I know the retelling of this story was supposed to make me feel better, but instead I felt worse than ever. My first day of high school simply wasn't meant to be a good one, and I questioned if I really did have the "inner strength" to turn things around.

* * *

A Dad's View

All teenagers have their nightmare days, their moments of angst and loneliness. It's a father's job to try and cheer them up, and I think the story of my wrestling match, and reminding Kristin of how she overcame past calamities really helped her. After my stories she went up to her room and probably slept like a baby.

There were so many stories I could have told her to make her feel better, and it's true what I said about how events in my teenage years and high school are still fresh in my mind. I could have told her about the time Steve Scatolini threw me out of the boys locker room and into a girls gym class stark naked. And I could have told her about the time I was Michael Barger's campaign manager for Class President and totally screwed up my speech before the entire ninth grade. And there was the time Coco Cannon stuffed my head in the toilet of the boy's room and kept flushing the damn thing during a break in the middle of the freshman dance.

Luckily, none of these left lasting scars... I think.

CHAPTER 3

A LOSING SEASON

The fall of my freshman year was extremely underwhelming. I dreaded the menacing beep of the alarm clock summoning me to rise and brace myself for the fifteen minute walk to the bus stop. As the weeks gave way from September to October, the temperature grew colder and my backpack grew heavier. I had myself convinced I was on my way to backpack-induced scoliosis. My classes were quite difficult, and all my courses were now nearing midterm exams. Being used to receiving A's and excelling in my middle school classes, my sub-par B grades that year did not help with my feeling of total mediocrity.

My social life was a C-plus at best, as the boys at school seemed to be interested in every girl in my group of friends except for me. Maybe it was because of the way I looked—my forehead was so shiny it served as a mirror for people wanting to catch their reflection when talking to me, while my eyebrows resembled fuzzy brown caterpillars that had been sloppily glued above my eyelids by a toddler, and there was no taming them. And my hair remained puffy and frizzy no matter how much product I soaked it in. To make matters worse, the much anticipated freshman dance was coming up in the spring, and my anxiety about not being asked by anyone to the dance had been mounting the moment I learned of it.

By November I felt completely buried in my academic and extracurricular responsibilities. I was still dancing five days a week and had decided to join the high school gymnastics team, where I only contributed to one of the four main events, that being the floor. I was initially attracted to the idea of being part of a new team with new girls to meet, but many of the team members ended up being current dancers I already knew. We choreographed our own routines to compete with, and I was a strong tumbler since my dance studio put an emphasis on being able to perform gymnastics tricks in our dance routines. But being bred a dancer versus a gymnast, I never did particularly well competing against girls who had been technically trained in gymnastics their entire lives. My floor routine scores consistently fell in the average to below average range, and after several meets with no signs of improvement, I stopped working as hard to perfect my routine and settled for average.

When I first considered joining the team my Dad said I could do so under one condition: I had to find someone to carpool with. He simply refused to drive me both ways to practice every week as my Mom worked as a nurse during the late afternoon and evening. I was mortified at the thought of having to ask friends to carpool, all of whom lived on the opposite side of town from me. Just as I expected, everyone's Moms declined my Dad's carpool proposition. I resorted to practically begging a girl on the team— someone named Tara I had known from dance—to carpool, and it was a hallelujah moment when her parents obliged.

I'm confident Tara regretted this arrangement after the first practice when it was my Dad's turn to pick us up. We saw his Subaru parked under a street light with my Dad standing by the trunk. Tara and I walked to the car, but there was no place for her to sit because the backseat was piled with fishing equipment, books, magazines, peanut jars, empty water bottles, and about two dozen other items that belonged hidden in a dark basement or kitchen cabinets. I pushed some things aside and Tara was able to cram herself in. I hopped in the front seat and we waited, shivering in the freezing-cold car, for my Dad to take his place in the driver's seat. That's when my Dad opened his door and said, "Shoot. I seem to have misplaced the keys. I just got back from a walk while waiting for you two."

For thirty frigid minutes we helped him sort through stacks of junk hunting for the keys. Irritated, shivering and embarrassed by this revolting car he fondly called his "mobile home," I said, "Dad, we would be off and driving by now if you cleaned your car out for once instead of making my friend and I suffer."

"I live out of this thing. This is how I make my living."

I found that hard to believe as I glanced at a recently dug up dogwood tree sapling protruding from the back of the car, then turned my gaze to a bag of decade old Halloween candy on the dashboard. I was going to snap back at him but bit my tongue not wanting to get into a fight in front of Tara. Instead I kept hunting for the keys, which I found *outside* the car, two feet beyond the front door laying in the middle of the parking lot.

"That's the strangest thing," my Dad said, "I have no idea how they got there. But at least we got my car a little better organized during the search."

On the drive home an odor spread through the car. "Dad, what's that smell?"

"Must be the corn on the cob and salmon I was eating in here for dinner," he said casually. "Some of the fish fell down between the seats but there is still a little in the tinfoil. You guys want some?"

Oh my God, he's serious, I thought. I was so embarrassed. Nightmarish thoughts of what Tara would tell her parents about her first carpool experience with us consumed me the entire ride.

* * *

I survived the carpooling arrangement, but other challenges awaited, namely the gymnastic leotards we had to wear. High cut leotards with no tights were a completely new territory for my dance friends and I on the gymnastics team, and being only a few years into puberty, we used what product seemed like the easiest and safest solution: Nair.

My introduction to Nair was, in a word, traumatic. Being a naive young teen not yet skilled in the way of hair removal, I thought it safe to leave the cream on for ten minutes longer than the directions said. The smell of the cream alone almost killed me when I tried it one fall afternoon before my first gymnastics meet, feeling faint from the fumes which reeked of chemicals. But I was determined. For twenty minutes I let the Nair cream work its magic. The first five minutes were uneventful. After seven minutes I felt a burning sensation, and thought, *this must mean it's working.* More burning ensued, and I thought, *Yes. This must be good. This pain is good.* Then after twenty minutes of searing, I winced a bit as I washed away all the cream, fully expecting to find I had the soft, smooth, flawless skin Nair advertised.

What I saw horrified me. It looked like I had a just ran through a field of poison ivy on top of a perilous chicken pox outbreak mixed with shingles. It was unlike any rash I had ever had in my life. I frantically searched the box and must have somehow missed the "DO NOT EXCEED 10 MINUTES" on the label. I was a Nair abomination and would be the joke of the gymnastics team.

I didn't compete in our first meet that day. It was like my Dad's wresting meet story was playing out in the context of my life. I told everyone I had come down with a stomach bug and sulked in the corner of the gym in discomfort and misery, never taking my sweatpants off, vowing to myself that I'd never use Nair again and I'd always follow directions. While packing up to leave, I let it slip to my friend Jess that I was not sick but had in fact burnt myself by excessive Nairing. By the time we returned to the high school, word of my catastrophe had spread throughout the bus, and before every meet that season someone would ask me if I Naired that day.

* * *

By the time Thanksgiving rolled around, I felt totally burnt out from the grind of honors classes, gymnastics and dance. Sometimes I didn't get home until eight or nine at night, famished and needing a shower. Nine o'clock onward was allocated solely to completing homework assignments, papers, and studying for exams before the holiday.

Needing a mental break one night from studying, I put down my biology book and headed to the kitchen for a snack. Brian had the same idea, only his snack break was not due to mental strain from schoolwork but from hours of exerting himself at PlayStation.

"Did you know they have a show about women who didn't know they were pregnant?" my Dad asked us casually from the kitchen table, where he was meticulously drawing a map of the

Gloucester shoreline for one of his books.

"Yea, it's pretty popular actually," I said bluntly. "They go to the bathroom to take a dump and instead a baby comes out."

"Out of her butt?" Brian stammered in disbelief.

Sensing the perturbed tone in my voice, my Dad asked me how I was holding up. "Not well," I replied somberly. "I just feel so swamped and stressed. Like I have so much to do and so little time to do it in."

Recognizing my anxiety, my Dad walked over to me and gave me a heartfelt hug, which instantly made me feel better. "All you can do is your best Kristin," he said. "Don't worry about the rest, it will all be fine. Remember, we're all just passing through."

We're all just passing through.

He was right. I had spent nearly every weeknight completely invested in my schoolwork, leaving little time to just *be*. Be fourteen. Be with my family. Be with my thoughts. I watched my Dad walk back to the kitchen table and sit down. How many nights would I have like this with him? The two of us in the same kitchen? Soon I would be in college, then working and living who knows where.

I scooped some cookie dough ice cream into a dish, and instead of turning to go upstairs, I pulled out the seat across from him and sat down.

* * *

Days later, Thanksgiving vacation was here and two of my favorite people in the world were visiting: my Grandpa and my Uncle Mark. During Thanksgiving dinner, I noticed my Grandpa wasn't taking part in the conversation, perhaps because at almost 80 years old he could barely hear, having lost most of his auditory skills to years of working at the Tougias family bakery in Springfield, MA. My great grandfather started the bakery after emigrating from Greece to America, and it was a source of family pride. My Grandpa would often tell us stories about the bakery, including how his father managed to keep the bakery alive and give bread to people in need during the Great Depression.

To communicate with my Grandpa, you had to be extremely loud and demonstrative.

"Grandpa!" I bellowed so loud it made everyone else at the dinner table jump.

With his mouth open and just about to take another bite of stuffing he halted, his fork suspended in front of his mouth.

"Yes?" he answered.

"I was just noticing how amazing your skin is. You don't have one wrinkle."

He put down the fork and smiled. "Thank you. But I have a big one right here," he said. He then leaned his body to the side so that he was practically hanging off his chair and pointed to his butt crack.

Shocked, all I could do was gasp. The family then simultaneously erupted into booming laughter. *No wonder Dad is so bizarre.*

My Grandpa went back to eating his meal as if nothing had happened. "Wow," he said inspecting his plate carefully as he chewed. "If the German army had this, they could have taken Russia!"

Later that night, my Dad went to call our Uncle Bob to wish him a Happy Thanksgiving. When he hung up, I asked him why he didn't let any of us talk and say Happy Thanksgiving as well.

Apparently soon after exchanging pleasantries, my Dad realized he was not on the phone with his brother. "I must have punched in a number of another person who is on my sheet of contacts I keep in my wallet," he explained. "Whoever I called had caller ID, so they knew who I was and started asking me about what book project I was working on. I thought maybe I'd recognize the voice, but I didn't. After we had been talking for five minutes I was too embarrassed to ask who I was speaking with."

"You mean you just kept the conversation going, and didn't have a clue who was on the other line?" I asked.

"Exactly. After ten minutes of me asking how they were doing —hoping they would give me a clue—I still had no idea which one of the 50 people on my contact list I was talking to. Then it got really embarrassing when there was a long pause and the person must have been waiting for me to explain the point of my call. I had to think fast, so I just said, "Well, I've missed you this past year, and I just wanted to let you know I was thinking of you. Happy Thanksgiving." The man on the phone was so taken aback, he said 'Wow. You know what, that is the nicest thing anyone has done in a long time. Thank you so much! You made my day.'"

I shook my head. "Something like that would only happen to you. You need to get a cell phone, I heard they can store your numbers on speed dial." It was 2002 and I did not yet have a cell phone, but some people at my high school had them. My Dad was on the house phone for business purposes all the time, so I dreamt of the day I would get my own cell and not have to compete with him for phone time.

"Kristin, what am I going to do with a cell phone? People will start calling me when I'm in the car, and that's the one time I feel totally relaxed."

I had no idea how anyone could feel remotely at peace in that car.

* * *

In the evening, my Grandpa, Mom, Dad, Uncle Mark, Brian and I were gathered in the family room to watch TV and compete against one another in Jeopardy. As we waited for Wheel of Fortune to end, my Dad broke the silence and said, "I think I saw Vanna White posing nude in a magazine once when I was waiting in the hospital for one of you kids to be born. She was hot."

"We should look that up," Brian said.

"Wait a minute," I said. "What were you doing looking at a magazine like that when one of your kids was about to be born?"

"I guess it was a slow period."

Now my Mom broke in, "Well that's nice to know. While I was in excruciating pain during labor, you were down in a newsstand checking out naked women."

This had the potential to derail what had been a fun and peaceful Thanksgiving. Most likely whatever my father said next would get him in further trouble. Brian bailed him out inadvertently, but only succeeded in getting my Dad in more hot water.

"Hey Dad, that reminds me, how about the time we looked for the topless donut shop we heard about on the radio one morning on our way fishing."

My Dad was about to speak but this time Alex Trebek saved him, as Jeopardy had begun.

"Quiet everyone!" he yelled, "It's time to play Jeopardy and this time I'm going to win!"

My Grandpa, roused by my Dad's shout, said, "Did you say it's time for a glass of gin?"

"No, no, we're playing Jeopardy."

"Well then turn the darn TV up," said my Grandpa. "And quit talking."

For once my Dad did as he was told. Halfway through Jeopardy I had a chocolate craving and went into the kitchen to grab a bag of Raisinets. I returned to join the rest of the family on the couch, all of whom were arguing about who got the last Jeopardy answer out first. I plopped back down on the couch, reached in the bag and emerged with a fistful of Raisinets, which I poured into my mouth like a truck dumping gravel.

"Kristin!" my Mom shrieked, looking utterly disgusted from the other end of the couch. "How can you possibly still be hungry? You gotta lay off the chocolate."

"It's fruit," I replied.

After a few moments of quiet, "God help me if you're 33 and single," she muttered.

I thought, *at this rate, I probably will be.*

When Jeopardy was over, my Grandpa went to resume reading his thousand page book *World War II, Volume VI*, but first said, "Hey Kristin, do some of those gymnastics tricks you showed me last year."

After swallowing a mouthful of what had to be one hundred plus Raisinets, I went into a handstand and came down quicker than usual, nervous I might barf on the living room carpet and be grounded. Our cat did it all the time, but she always got away with it.

"I can do that," my Dad said. He then got off the couch, went onto his hands and knees, and entered a headstand. Immediately upon raising his legs, dozens of coins began to tumble out of his pockets and scattered across the living room floor. "NO!" he yelled as he lost his balance, crashing down on his back with the grace of an elephant, and rolled over onto his stomach with his arms desperately flailing across the floor trying to gather the change still rolling in every direction.

"Serves you right," said my Grandpa laughing. "Don't try to show off you old man!"

And so it went the rest of the night, a mix of bickering, good-natured humor, and gymnastics. A typical Thanksgiving at the Tougias homestead.

* * *

The next day, my Mom went for a power walk around our block. On her way back, a neighbor spotted her and flagged her over to talk. He told her how pleased he was that my Dad thought to call him and wish him a happy Thanksgiving. So moved by my Dad's gesture, he said it was one of the nicest things anyone had done in a long time.

Little did he know it was a total accident.

Although he will if he reads this book.

* * *

In December, things at school became a bit more comfortable as I knew my way around the high school. But lunches were still a dread, and I spent many precious minutes searching desperately for a table with some friends. Because I was one of the few people who brought my lunch every day, I was usually the first to sit down while everyone waited in line for chicken nuggets and mashed potatoes. Since no one was ever looking for *me*, the first person out of the lunch line would stake their place at some other table, typically one I was not seated at, and I would have to move and casually pull out a chair, acting as though I had just entered the lunchroom. We had less than 20 minutes to eat—18 minutes to be exact—which basically bought me just enough time to wolf down a sandwich and then scurry off to English where the teacher was fixated on dissecting *Lord of the Flies* in every way possible, making me want to regurgitate my lunch long before it was digested. But lunch did have one bright side, and that was an encouraging daily note my Mom would enclose with my homemade turkey and swiss sandwich, often complete with a sketch of our cat, Casper.

On Friday, my biology teacher announced that the next few weeks of class would be spent constructing our major class project, a "bio-dome." This container would be constructed from scratch and then monitored for a few months, ultimately leading up to one important grade. The class was divided into groups of four. Luckily I had Michelle in that class with me, so we automatically knew we would be partners. But finding two other girls was not as easy. In the end, we were forced to group with three boys who were unable to find an additional partner. I hated working with boys because I usually ended up doing all the work.

The remainder of the class was spent working in our groups designing our bio-dome, which had to be successful in sustaining life. It needed some sort of aquatic section and a dry section. We came up with the idea of putting a wall in the middle of the container to separate the water from the soil, with holes in the middle to act as pores to permeate the soil and grow the grass.

That weekend we all had to buy the materials and organisms for the bio-dome and come back to class Monday ready to begin building. My Dad was excited to offer me supplies, for he took a particular interest in gardening. It was quite common to come home from school on a spring afternoon and find him toiling away in his vegetable garden, planting seeds and arranging plots. The worst part was, he would wear no shirt and a 1980's Celtics hat with an oversized, flat brimmed green bill that stuck out like a huge beak. It looked ridiculous with his large glasses and dirt-stained gardening gloves, but he worked with such pride that the ensemble didn't seem to bother him in the least. Not that his ensembles ever did. And on particularly hot days, he would break out a light purple belly shirt he cut himself, exposing his bellybutton-less gut for all the world to see.

When I told him that I needed to bring in soil, the only bag he had was king-sized and gigantic. I feared it slipping out of my hands it in the hallway and becoming "the girl who dropped a bunch of dirt in main hall." The next day, however, found me carrying the sack of soil like a massive baby through my whole neighborhood and onto the bus. I plopped it down in the seat next to me, and I heard someone yell from the back seat, "Oh Kristin, is a sack of dirt your new bus buddy?" Carrying it through main hall was even more embarrassing: hard as I tried, there was simply no way to look cool hefting a huge sack of dirt through the halls of my high school.

Constructing the bio-dome was a stressful process. We had to cut plexiglass, super-glue a tank together, build the wall in the middle, insert the soil and plant the seeds, get water to stay in the "pond" section without leaking, add snails, fish and a salamander, and complete a write up about its success at the very end. The first twenty minutes of every class would be spent assessing the bio dome. This included checking PH levels, taking photos of the soil to count every blade of grass, monitoring the organisms, and so on. Each form of life counted as a certain number of points. The more blades of grass, the more points you received. The bigger the animal and the longer it lived, the more it counted for. Michelle and I calculated practically everything because the boys were too busy goofing off. It seemed the only thing their brains were capable of at that time was counting grass.

Things started off promising: the bio-dome buzzed with life as our salamander, who we fondly named Salamander Steve, crawled and grass began to grow. But this was extremely short lived. The blades of grass withered and died. The fish began to die off one by one as PH levels spiraled out of control. Despite my efforts to revive the bio-dome and regain control of the environment, the project was doomed, and so was Salamander Steve, who passed shortly thereafter.

Devastated by the inevitable failure of this assignment and what was sure to be an atrocious grade, the loss of life and the death of Salamander Steve, bio class became depressing. Just when I thought it couldn't get any worse, I arrived for class one day and my teacher called our group over to his desk. He looked tired and annoyed. "Yesterday evening, your bio-dome burst," he informed us. "I spent the night cleaning and saved the few intact pieces of the tank for you," he said, gesturing to the windowsill to his right. "You'll have to come after school and rebuild it in your own time. I don't know what this will mean for your project as a whole, but I can assure you if you leave it in this condition, you'll receive an F."

The release of the letter "F" left his mouth and hit me like a bullet. I felt myself go weak in the knees and the room began to spin. "We will rebuild!" I shouted with the same resolve as a political leader whose country had been attacked.

I was met with the awful smell of death and decay as I walked to what was left of our bio-dome. It was a sad heap of glass and dirt and rocks our teacher had put off to the side of the room in a plastic container. The next day I hauled onto the bus yet another heavy bag of soil and was met with more scrutinizing stares as I carried the sack once again through main hall.

At the end of the school day I went to my locker where I had stored the bag, ready to rebuild the bio-dome. I must have pierced the bag at some point during the day by carelessly jamming it into my locker and throwing my books on top of it, because when I opened my locker, a fast-flowing stream of dirt came pouring onto my new camel-colored suede clogs and onto the floor around me.

Needless to say, we did not receive a good grade for this disaster of a project, which became more of a death trap than a house for life. By the time the assignment deadline hit, my bio-dome had performed worst in the class. Luckily the teacher gave us a C-minus, but the project was 30 percent of our grade, and I thought this would sink my chance of making the honor roll.

That evening when I returned home feeling defeated, I kicked off my dirt-smeared clogs in the hallway and they landed next to my Dad's decrepit gardening shoes. I let out a big sigh—the two pairs of shoes looked identical.

* * *

In early Spring I decided to try out for softball, having played every year since third grade. I made the freshman team, and my coach happened to be my former seventh grade homeroom teacher who now taught history at the high school. On the first day of practice, Mr. Wayne sat all the girls down and introduced himself.

"Now, you're probably asking yourselves what my credentials are as a softball coach. The answer is I have none. But I've coached my son's T-ball team and I watch the Red Sox, so that makes me qualified." I wasn't sure I agreed with that statement, but I really liked Mr. Wayne and had built a good rapport with him years ago. I was to start at second base and was thrilled.

It was a sunny spring day when we took to the field for our first practice. The freshman dance was just one week away, and I was the last girl in my group of friends to be asked to the dance. Other girls were taking boys in the grade above us, since it was much cooler to be going to the dance with a sophomore than a freshman. My situation was looking bleak until a guy friend named Tim—who I'd been told had a crush on me—asked me to go with him in a handwritten card. I checked the box that said "yes" and handed it back to him after last period.

Thinking about the upcoming dance made it hard to focus on softball practice, but I fared better than another girl on my team.

Mr. Wayne stood at home plate with a bucket of softballs at his side to hit to those of us in the field. He grabbed a fresh white softball, tossed it in front of him and smacked it. The pop up soared through the air to left center field, where a girl I had gone to middle school with was standing.

"I got it!" she screamed with her glove stretched in front of her, but something didn't look right. She held her arm out directly in front of her, parallel to her chest rather than up above her head, where the ball was about to land and where her head was facing. I gasped as I watched the softball land squarely on her face. She dropped to the ground and writhed in pain while clutching her face in her hands.

Mr. Wayne threw down his bat and muttered "shit!" as he ran by me towards the outfield, and the rest of us followed. "Someone get the nurse. Practice is over!" he yelled and waved us all away. The poor girl would have to go to her first high school formal with a bruised and battered face, and I knew this couldn't be a good sign of the season to come.

After school, my Mom took me dress shopping at our local mall for the upcoming dance. I chose a slim fitting light green sparkly dress, with two straps and a low back. I then bought two Swarovski crystal sparkly barrettes, deciding I would wear my hair down, parted down the middle with a section on both sides pulled back in the front by the clips. No one told me I'd regret that hair decision years later.

On the night of the dance I was a nervous wreck. I was running behind because dance practice went over the time allotted. When my Mom and I pulled into the driveway, I dashed out of the car and sprinted up the stairs into the bathroom to shower, wash, and blow-dry my hair, which was always a production as my hair was frizzy and unmanageable. I had just enough time to put on some mascara and eyeliner before my date and his parents arrived at our house. I was feeling tense with two sets of parents watching me attempt to pin on his corsage, which I totally botched, some petals falling off the white rose in my attempts to secure it to his suit. Tim then slipped the corsage onto my wrist, and our parents took an absurd amount of pictures of the two of us. *Jeeze, we're not getting married,* I thought. Then he and I got in the back of his Dad's car and set out for the high school cafeteria.

Once at the dance I couldn't relax, especially because several teachers were there as chaperones. There is something so unnatural about seeing your teachers in any context outside of the classroom, and I felt extremely awkward dancing with Tim in front of them.

* * *

The softball season was an absolute disaster win-wise, because we lost every single game. At our second-to-last game, Mr. Wayne invited his entire family to watch. This included his wife, his young children, and his in-laws. In the first play of the game, a girl on the opposite team ripped a grounder and it went right between my legs. Shortly after, another batter hit a line drive to my right which I dove for and missed. In the same inning I bobbled a ground ball which should have been an easy out but instead resulted in a run scored by the other team. Mr. Wayne had seen enough and benched me for the rest of the game. "What is going on with you today, Kristin!" he yelled.

The truth was I had received a C on an English project because my partner handed in his portion in blue colored pencil when it was supposed to be typed. To make myself feel better I ate three cookies, a bag of Doritos and four packs of gushers on the bus ride and consequently played like total crap as a result of eating and feeling like crap. I sulked on the bench while his extended family watched in horror as the other team piled on runs. We lost 21-0, and Mr. Wayne was silent the entire bus ride back.

While the team itself was no assembly of all-star softball players, I became quite close with a few of the girls, especially a girl named Erin who shared my love for sarcastic humor. We got through the season by entertaining our teammates with free-style rap on the bus rides and sometimes even in the dugout. Our teammates loved our rap competitions and would gather around us chanting and applauding. As the season drew to a close, none of us were focused on softball. Even when our team was in the field it was not uncommon to see some of the girls drawing pictures in the dirt in the middle of an inning.

As a special treat and probably the only appropriate way he knew to celebrate a losing season, Coach Wayne promised to take us to Burger King after the last game, win or lose. We were pumped. Maybe it was the promise of fried food, but for whatever reason, our team played well for the first time ever. We were up by one run in the bottom of the last inning, and finally it seemed a win was at hand. The other team was at bat with two outs and one girl on first base. Victory was painfully close.

Then Mr. Wayne made a curious substitution, involving the girl on our team who had been hit in the face on the first day of practice. Because of her injury she wore a catcher's mask the entire season as precaution. Due to a mix of fear and inability to see from behind so many bars, she missed most of the balls that came to her in the outfield, so most of the time she sat the bench. In the last inning, Mr. Wayne decided to let her play left field, and as fate would have it, the next batter hit a bomb her way. Her glove was nowhere near the ball. It soared past her and further into the outfield, resulting in a homerun. The game was lost.

Erin and I decided to break the tense silence and kill time on the bus ride to Burger King by orchestrating some pranks, one of which involved having a really timid and unassuming girl on the team ask Mr. Wayne for something embarrassing. All the softball girls were crowded in the last ten rows of the back of the bus while Mr. Wayne sat in the very front seat behind the driver, strategically situating himself as far from us as possible. "Mr. Wayne," the shy girl shouted from the back. All of us held our breath and suppressed giggles before she asked, "Do you have a tampon?" Mr. Wayne turned scarlet, shook his head and turned around. All the softball girls erupted into hysterics, and Erin and I went into Burger King feeling mischievous.

After all the orders for burgers and chicken fingers and fries were placed, we sat down and spread out among six different tables, with Mr. Wayne sitting solo in another attempt to distance himself from twenty obnoxious teenage girls. Erin and I then devised our next plan. We knew that at any moment, Mr. Wayne would be delivering his post-game speech, followed by the naming of the game MVP. After every game, Mr. Wayne gave credit to someone new who made a great play, or more commonly in our case since we were so bad, had a "winning attitude." The MVP got whatever toy Mr. Wayne swiped from his toddler's McDonald's Happy Meal that week. He stood before us and asked us all to be please be quiet and listen up, as he had a few closing remarks regarding the season.

"Now, I know we weren't the best team in the league," he began. "Actually, we were the worst. But that doesn't matter. What matters is—" Mr. Wayne's speech came to a screeching halt as I stood up from my chair and walked directly over to him, exaggeratedly outstretching my arms, and encased him in a big hug. I heard giggling and clapping from my teammates behind me, and Mr. Wayne was completely speechless as I pulled away. He shook his head and stood there, probably trying to collect himself and continue his speech. After a minute, he must have decided to heck with the MVP selection and pep talk, knowing by now our team had the attention span of twenty puppies. "This season certainly had a lot of interesting moments ... and continues to. It was a pleasure to be your coach."

When the meals came, Erin and I executed our next prank. Erin walked over to the other side of the restaurant to use the bathroom. As she exited and made her way back over to our group of tables, she passed the long line of Burger King customers. Something at Erin's feet caused every single person in line to look down at her and send her glances of outrage. Once again we all started laughing, and I watched Mr. Wayne pick his head up from his burger to see what all the commotion was about. Unable to see her feet, Mr. Wayne looked perplexed. But as Erin rounded the corner and came into view, there it was—nearly an entire roll of toilet paper stuck to her cleat, dragging behind her and making a trail across the Burger King floor like a wedding veil. This caused my teammates to collapse in such a fit of hysteria that for a brief moment I was nervous we would be kicked out before having the chance to finish our value meals.

Mr. Wayne shook his head for a third time that afternoon and went back to eating his burger, probably thankful that he had chosen a fast food spot versus a longer sit-down venue. But between bites of his Whopper, I could see him laughing.

* * *

A Dad's View

Kristin's softball season may have been a disaster, but I felt a newfound sense of pride in my daughter. Not for her athletic skills, but for making the best out of a bad situation. Toward the end of the season she would come home from each loss with a smile. I'd ask her if her team finally won, and she shook her head. "Then why so happy?" I'd ask. Kristin would tell me about some rap song or prank that she and Erin had concocted, and I thought that truly is the way to handle adversity. Laugh it off. I wish I had done more of that when I was in high school, especially while on the soccer team. I was voted co-captain by my fellow players, but I was probably the slowest kid on the team. The darn coach barely let me play for more than two or three minutes a game, and if it was a close contest in the second half, I never even got off the bench. The biggest sweat I worked up was before the game when I'd jog out to the center of the field and shake hands with the referees and opposing team's captains. Those games were miserable for me. School sports should be about every team member playing, getting plenty of exercise and having a good time, winning should be secondary. I'm glad Mr. Wayne let the girls have fun; he knew something few school coaches ever understand.

Now about my car: it's true the thing was a mess, but the way I look at it there are two types of car owners. There are those who baby their car, and feel the hunk of steel and plastic is a reflection of their personality, consequently their vehicle is always spotless on the inside and shiny on the outside. Then there are those of us who think of our cars as merely a way to get from point A to B; we beat the hell out of them, go a full year without changing the oil, and keep whatever we think we might need inside the vehicle. It is amazing all the items you may someday need while driving. So for a busy guy like me having my car stocked with "stuff" makes sense.

I've shaved in my car, flossed my teeth, and someday I'll undoubtedly wash my hair while driving down Route 128. And like everyone else I eat in my car. While others buy fast food that will kill them slowly, I prefer to bring healthy leftovers from home. You are what you eat, which explains why I was munching on corn on the cob and salmon the day I was waiting for Kristin to finish gymnastics practice. Something was bound to spill—in my case it was the salmon, and I am truly sorry for that, so sorry I'm going to invent the "car bib"—a large protective towel that is fastened to the seat belt. Every time you enter the car and buckle your seat belt your chest and lap will be protected from spilled coffee, butter sliding off corn on the cob, and greasy fish. Wait till Kristin's friends see it for the first time, they will beg their parents to get one too. Practicality beats style any day, and I'll bet you too will soon be wearing the car bib.

CHAPTER 4

THE SHARK ENCOUNTER

At the end of my freshman year I was shocked when my father announced our next family trip. This vacation idea was totally out of character for him. It was not a freebie, as in not another North Lake Resort, but to Maui, as in Maui, Hawaii. My father explained his thinking this way: "We all love to snorkel, and Maui's got some of the best anywhere. We need one awesome family vacation before you kids don't want to go on vacation with me anymore. I can also write up an article about Hawaii to pitch to The New York Times or The Globe."

I didn't have the heart to tell him that after North Lake Resort, neither Brian nor I wanted to go anywhere with him again. But I could make an exception for Hawaii.

And so within just one month of my Dad announcing this grand vacation, the four of us found ourselves in Maui. School was out, summer had begun, and we were having a blast. Snorkeling really was the glue that kept us in agreement for extended periods of time together. My Dad had researched the best snorkeling spots in a great guidebook titled *Maui Revealed*, and he had us on a mission to snorkel 10 different spots in our 12-day vacation. Surprisingly, I loved the idea. But on the final day of the trip, we may have snorkeled one too many times.

* * *

It was another picture-perfect morning in Maui as I leapt out of bed to eat some cereal before the family drove to a new secluded beach to snorkel. These early morning excursions had become standard on our vacation; we would wake up around eight o'clock and be out of our condo by nine in order to beat the building winds that whipped Maui's coast. These winds created large surf and decreased water visibility, making it increasingly difficult to snorkel and avoid being bashed into the surrounding coral. We drove to a beach that was said to be a favorite among sea turtles, and I couldn't wait to swim with these creatures that had fascinated me since I was a little girl.

I had always loved turtles, owning quite a few painted turtle pets when I was young. Oftentimes we would find them while swimming in a pond, keep them for a couple of weeks and then return them to their natural habitat. Yet these turtles were about the size of a softball, and usually scattered whenever humans were around, so the thought of a calm, gentle and giant sea turtle with a shell three feet in diameter intrigued me. In fact swimming with sea turtles in the wild was one of my ultimate dreams, along with dolphins and manatees.

When we arrived at the beach, I swiftly slid on my flippers and secured my mask over my face. To my dismay, I woke up that morning to find my period had just begun, and I knew it would be a hassle to be at the beach. About a year prior, I had one of the worst welcome-to-womanhood experiences a girl going through puberty could ever endure: I was on stage in front of hundreds of people for my dance studio's rendition of The Nutcracker. About midway through my first number, composed of twenty girls in pure white rhinestone encrusted costumes, I noticed that with every leap, turn, split and kick, something on me was catching the eye of my fellow dancers, causing their overstated stage smiles to slant in an outraged way. It wasn't until the four-minute number ended when as I was gracefully exiting the stage that a group of three older girls grabbed me in the dark stage wing. "Kristin," one of them hissed, "do you realize that you got your period everywhere during the middle of that dance? In front of everyone?" I turned the color of that white costume as the blood drained from my face. I was officially a woman, and I was mortified.

In the back of my mind, I wondered if a shark would be attracted to me snorkeling because of this. I remembered watching television programs featuring divers who would put themselves in the middle of the ocean accompanied by a bloody hunk of fish meat, and within minutes 20 sharks would appear out of the blue depths to find its source. I approached my Dad in the condo's kitchen, who was agitatedly trying to cram his large flippers into a backpack.

"Hey Dad," I said uncomfortably, "do you think having my....ah...my period would have any effect on sharks?"

After what felt like an eternity of awkward silence for me and deep thought for him, he said not to worry, and with that I pushed the thought out of my mind.

We decided the search for turtles would be a family affair, and all four of us dove into the turquoise water together. Where the public beach ended was no boundary for us—the guide book mentioned the turtles could be found in a remote area of reef, and we quickly passed a point where a jumble of rocks jutted outwards, separating our beach from the unknown. The water was between ten and fifteen feet deep, and there was both coral and rock jutting up from the bottom, almost reaching the surface.

Visibility was crystal clear and I could see 30 feet in all directions, scanning the nooks and crannies of large rocky masses for a sea turtle.

It was about this time that my Mom's mask began to leak and she found a place to stand to correct it. Realizing that the place my mother had planted her feet was on coral, Brian over-reacted and made a quick decision to push her off. She was fixing her mask, then instantly lost balance and was unexpectedly in water over her head.

The yelling began as soon as my mother bobbed to the surface.

"BRIAN!" my mother shouted after coughing and spitting out a mouthful of seawater. "Why did you do that? What are you thinking?"

"You were standing on the coral!" Brian exclaimed. "You're not supposed to stand on the coral, it kills it!"

"So you pushed me off..."

My mother seemed at a loss for words. Not being a strong swimmer, she was completely unnerved by being suddenly shoved. Then she began to cry.

Here was our happy little family, out at sea, with my mother sobbing, my father trying to process the situation, my brother making his defense in the name of coral, and me thinking *here we go*.

"Kristin, you take Mom back to the beach," my father said. As we swam back in, my mother cursed what a stupid move Brian had made pushing her and how immature his actions had been. While I might have done something to save the coral from my mom's flippers, I would have used words rather than actions. It was a foolish move by Brian, and I was back on the sand paying for it. When I had finally calmed my Mom down ten minutes later, my Dad and Brian were returning. I feared the worst. *They've already seen a sea turtle,* I thought, *and by now it's probably halfway to Japan after having likely been chased by Brian.*

Sure enough. "We saw a sea turtle!" Brian bellowed.

"Great," I said. "Who knows when I'll get the chance to see one."

"Come on," my father said, "I'll take you and mom back out there, and Brian can stay with our things."

Brian made his case for the coral to my mother, and he gave his apology for pushing her off the rock. Still a bit flustered, she accepted his apology and she waded into the water with my father and me.

I swam ahead of my parents, looking every which way in hopes of catching a glimpse of the sun's rays hitting the shell of a round creature. I had my father bring the underwater camera just in case, and we made our way past the public beach off toward the rock point. The area was full of colorful coral and large masses of black lava rock that originated 20 feet below and sculpted their way up to the surface. I swam around them rapidly, hoping to meet a sea turtle on the other side. Still no luck. I looked behind me and found my parents lagging about 20 feet behind, and proceeded onward.

Next I arrived at a beautiful spot where two towering formations of coral covered rock stood side by side, creating a sort of passageway in the middle. As I approached this opening and swam inside I finally found what I had been so desperately searching for. Not just one, but four sea turtles were gracefully swimming around this coral haven, munching the algae from its edges. It was absolutely breathtaking to see such large, wild creatures in their natural setting. I glided further into their watery realm, and now the turtles were just two or three feet from me. They seemed as curious about me as I was about them, and I quickly poked my head up out of the water to flash my parents four fingers, signaling what I had just found.

I was swimming among the turtles now, side by side, maneuvering through the masses of coral and small fish. The current was noticeably stronger here; we were near the very tip of an outcropping of rock that also caused the ocean's surface to be a bit rough. There was one turtle I was following in particular, and I swam over its large shell in hopes that my father would capture a picture of the turtle and me. It began to head out into the open water. I lifted my head to the surface, where my father pulled off his mask and said, "Dive down and try to get closer to the turtle. I'll get a picture."

This is going to be amazing I thought. *An underwater picture of myself alongside a giant sea turtle.*

As the turtle glided downward into the blue depths, I took a deep breath and quickly dove into the water to follow behind. While swimming, I turned around and noticed that my father was not yet taking the picture—his head was still above water perhaps adjusting his mask. Still holding my breath, I turned back around and kicked aggressively in an effort to catch up with the turtle now fading out of view into the gloomy depths.

Suddenly, something off to the right caught my eye. What appeared to be a large shadow ominously emerged from behind the rocks. It was grey and about seven feet in length.

Oh my God. A shark.

The shark swam near the ocean's bottom, just ten feet away, circling under my father who couldn't see it. Now the full impact of what was happening hit me, and a shot of adrenaline coursed through my body, causing me to whip around and frantically swim to the surface. I ripped my mask off in a frenzy, looking over at my parents who had just dunked their heads in the water. I frantically motioned with my hands for them to surface and they did, swimming toward me.

"Did you see that shark below Dad?" I nervously called out.

"There's a shark!" my mother screamed.

"How big was it?" asked my father seriously.

I had a decision to make. I was on the verge of panic, and was certain the wrong choice of words could put my mother over the edge.

"Oh, not big," I said as coolly as possible, remembering my mother's incessantly verbalized fear of having a shark round the corner as she was snorkeling. "But we need to get out of here," I added with a greater sense of urgency this time.

I thought I was doing the right thing at the time, acting like it was no big deal to prevent my mother from freaking out. There was virtually no where to go; we were a long way from the shore of a barren beach, surrounded by coral and rocks impossible to climb or hide behind, and too far for any person to hear our screams. But my composed attitude and cool tone would prove to do the opposite of what I had intended.

Indeed, my mother did stay calm as we started swimming towards the direction of the beach. Yet when I turned around to make sure my father was behind us, my hopes of us swiftly making it back were shattered. He was snorkeling directly back to the spot where I saw the shark.

It occurred to me that I should have known by now that my Dad would react in such a way. Always curious, he wanted to see what he thought was a very small shark.

I called out to him, but he didn't hear. Instead I watched his back arch as he started to dive downward, his flippers emerging from the water as his body went from a horizontal position to a vertical one. I felt a wave of nausea sweep over me, thinking the image of his flippered-feet in the air might be the last I ever saw of him.

I held my breath, looking at the empty patch of ocean where he had dove. *Come on, come on*, I prayed. *Come back up! This is all my fault, I attracted the shark then told my Dad it was little.*

My mother had now stopped swimming, and looked back at me. "What's wrong?" she asked, with an edge in her voice.

"It's Dad, he dove down where the shark was."

My mother looked confused, probably wondering why I looked so upset if the shark was puny. She was about to say something when I saw my father's head pop up.

"Dad!" I screamed.

He looked at me, and I made an urgent motion with my arm signaling him to come to our location. For a moment he just stared at me with a dumb look on his face. He started to turn back again to where he thought the shark might have swum.

"Dad!" I yelled again. "Get out of there!"

He swiveled in the water, glancing back at me. Something about my scream must have registered, because now he started swimming toward me.

I stared at him, thinking at any moment I'd see a grey fin slice the water's surface behind him.

When he was next to my mother and me, he started to talk. "Why are you..."

I interrupted him, "Just get back to the beach fast!"

I feverishly swam toward shore, wanting to get there as

quickly as possible while simultaneously trying not to make any big splashes. My body was saying flee, yet my mind was saying slow down and stay calm.

I glanced over my shoulder toward my parents. My mother was ten feet behind me, and my Dad was at least 30 feet further out, taking his sweet time. Typical. I shouted for them to speed it up while pointing toward shore, and then I continued swimming. Of course, they had no idea the shark was as large as it was. While continuing at their leisurely pace, my Dad occasionally dove downward to inspect a piece of coral or a brightly colored fish.

The swim back to the beach seemed like an eternity. When I was finally able to touch my flippers to the sand, I pulled off my mask, and waited for my parents. My mother arrived first.

"I just lied to you," I said in shaky, out-of-breath voice.

"What?"

"I lied. That wasn't a small shark I saw, it was huge. I didn't want you to panic, so I had to say it was small. But it was scary."

"You're kidding!" she shouted, her eyes wide with terror.

"Nope. It was bigger than us, at least seven feet. I think it was attracted to us because of my period."

My mother and I both turned around to get my father's attention. He was still snorkeling like he hadn't a care in the world. We shouted at him, but he seemed not to hear. He was displaying himself like a Christmas ham, and it was a miracle he was not yet inside a shark's stomach.

When my father finally arrived, I told him I had lied about the shark being small.

"What?" he asked. "How big was it?"

"About seven feet. I was swimming down toward the turtle so you could take the picture, and as I was moving deeper I saw this huge shark come from around the corner and then circle under you."

The color drained from his face. He shook his head as if in disbelief then said, "But you sounded so calm when I asked how big it was!"

"I know, I know, I thought it would be the best thing to do! I remembered Mom, and how yesterday she kept saying she was afraid of seeing a shark while snorkeling. I didn't want her to panic!"

"What about me!" my father yelled. "I went back to look for it! I figured it was only a foot long because you acted so nonchalant." He stared at me accusingly. "I could have been torn to shreds!"

* * *

Later that day, we met a woman on the beach, and my Dad told her about what had happened while snorkeling. The woman looked at him with disbelief saying, "Wow … that's odd! I live here in Maui and snorkel all around the beach every day. But *never* have I seen a single shark, let alone a big one." Then the woman looked at me and smiled, saying, "What you saw is very special, even magical, something the rest of us will probably never experience."

My Dad didn't quite view the experience as special or magical. In fact during the rest of our Maui vacation, I often heard my father muttering to himself, "Oh, it's not very big."

When I returned home I told my friends what happened, and they thought the entire event was hysterical. But all I could think about was how I almost got my Dad killed—eaten by a shark of all the ways to go. But I know he didn't hold the incident against me, because I heard him tell a neighbor the shark story when we returned home, and both of them were laughing their heads off.

I'm still not sure what was more traumatic—the day I became a woman or the day I saw that shark.

* * *

A Dad's View

The trouble with teenagers is they usually stretch the truth, add drama, and generally embellish the mundane. How was I to know that the one time in my life I could be saved by an exaggeration, my daughter would do the opposite and understate what she saw?

After the incident, while still in Hawaii, I did a little research on sharks, and came to the conclusion that the seven-footer could have been a gray reef shark or a tiger shark. Now I know shark attacks are rare, and I've even seen a statistic that indicates that more people are killed by falling coconuts than by sharks, but that gave me little comfort. The book I skimmed about sharks and the Hawaiian Islands didn't help my new-found fear. It said: "Tiger sharks come near shore to prey on turtles. When the sun is hitting the water and the surface is rough, a shark cannot always differentiate between a turtle and a human. There have been a number of attacks on humans."

I remember a chill ran down my spine reading those words, then I replayed the snorkeling scene in my mind. The choppy water, the bright sunshine, and turtles all around us, followed by Kristin's motion for me to surface and our subsequent conversation. I could hear myself asking Kristin, "How big was the shark?" and her lackadaisical answer, "Oh, not big."

She might as well have rung the shark dinner bell, knowing I'd want to see the little fellow. Was she truly trying to keep my wife calm, or did she have something more sinister in mind? She had been complaining about how other kids have "normal" fathers...

CHAPTER 5

THE FIRST JOB — "SERVE THE F'IN ICE CREAM"

Almost everyone has something that helps them unwind at the end of the day; a glass of wine, watching mindless television, listening to music, or in my case, having a bowl of ice cream. As far back as I can remember I've had ice cream every night before bed. I looked forward to it all day—the other meals were simply a means of putting fuel in my body. And going out for ice cream was the ultimate treat, so naturally I thought working at an ice cream store would be the perfect first job. I'd be surrounded by my favorite food, and during slow periods with few customers I could serve myself instead.

I learned about an opening for this supposed dream job at the beginning of the summer just after our family vacation to Maui. A new ice cream store was going to open in a shopping plaza not far from my home, so my best friend, Kristine, and I decided to apply together. This would be my first job, and I was ecstatic. I thought, what could be better than working with ice cream and people my age?

Kristine and I drove to the new store location and walked into a large, empty, dusty white room. Through an open door in the back hallway we could see a truck and four people unloading boxes to be stacked against the back wall. She and I stood there— the only sound breaking the silence was the jingling of my car keys as I took one step forward then stopped, unsure of who to approach. Finally a young woman bringing in a box noticed us, put the box down and smiled as she power-walked to the front of the store to greet us. She was in her late twenties, with shoulder length auburn hair, wearing jeans and a red t-shirt that said "Sweetcone." "Hi," she said, "Are you looking for job applications?"

"Yeah," we both nodded excitedly. The woman walked over to a folder that lay on the floor to the right of us. She squatted down, grabbed two application sheets and handed them to us with an overzealous grin.

"Here you go! Just bring these back here when you're done. Tryouts will be two weeks from now."

Tryouts? I thought. *Why would I possibly need to try out for an ice cream shop?* An interview seemed plausible, but tryouts were for things like sports teams. Or so I thought.

I handed my application in the next day, and two weeks later found myself sitting in the same large white room with about twenty other high school kids, including Kristine, all of us slightly perplexed as to what we had to do to serve ice cream here. Did you have to be athletic? Good-looking? Would they measure my bicep on my scooping arm?

Waves of anxiety swept over me as I stared at the pubescent zit-infested faces surrounding me. The twenty or so applicants were in chairs arranged in a circle, and we all shot nervous glances at each other. Three Sweetcone officials, two males and a female, stood off to the side sorting through the applications. One man walked over to the edge of the circle and bellowed, "Hi guys, how's everyone doing today!" He was short, about my height, and looked more like a fitness instructor than the owner of an ice cream shop. He wore a tight collared t-shirt with the Sweetcone logo above the left breast, and he had more energy than a seven-year-old on a sugar high.

We all responded to his question with a thunderous and drawn out, "Goooood!"

He clapped his hands once before speaking again.

"Welcome to what will soon be the newest Sweetcone ice cream parlor. I'm Mitch, this is Jasper, and this is Marsha. Jasper is a member of our design team and he will also be assisting us with training. Marsha will be the manager of this store, while I'll be back and forth between here and my other Sweetcone store."

Sitting to Mitch's right was Jasper, a vibrant looking twenty-something year old guy with tight black curls and green eyes. He was holding a pen over a pad of paper as he flashed his white teeth to a circle of anxious faces. To Mitch's left was Marsha, an extremely large woman in her early thirties, with incredibly short boy-cut, reddish blonde hair and black-rimmed glasses. She looked irritated, like she'd rather be anywhere on earth but encased in this circle of hormone raging teens, which made her instantly intimidating to all.

Mitch, Marsha and Jasper scanned the circle of eager faces staring back at them. We waited for some sort of instruction. After what felt like a decade of watching their probing eyeballs dart around the sea of anxious oily faces hoping to make minimum wage, Mitch asked us each to give our names, where we were from, and one interesting fact about ourselves. Since I was sitting directly to the left of the store manager Marsha, he asked me to go first. I felt my face go red, but I plunged right in, trying to match Mitch's enthusiasm.

"Hi everyone, I'm Kristin, I'm going to be a sophomore and, umm...." My voice trailed off as I thought hard about what made me unique. *I have a bunion? No that's gross. I used to be obsessed with the Oregon Trail? No that's weird.*

Then it came to me.

"I can walk on my hands."

Mitch asked if I would demonstrate. With all eyes in the room on me, I stood up and stuffed my shirt into my jeans as far as I could to keep my stomach and bra from showing. I took a few steps away from my chair and toward the center of the circle to prevent kicking Marsha in the face on my way down, stared at the dusty white floor, and then went into a handstand. I balanced for a moment, and then began taking steps forward with my hands. I heard a "wow," stood back up and was met with a light applause. I can only imagine how red the combination of attention mixed with being upside down made my face.

Throughout these "tryouts" Mitch asked people to give him a glimpse of what made them special. Some were downright weird. One kid said he could hold his breath underwater for two minutes (as if he could ever prove that here), and one girl said she had a collection of pet grasshoppers. Seriously.

When we got to the end of the circle, Mitch proceeded to give us a brief overview of the Sweetcone vision. He then went on to explain what they look for in a Sweetcone employee: "We only want responsible, friendly, and above all extremely enthusiastic people to serve our customers. And so begins another round of auditions."

A sense of dread overwhelmed me. *Another round of auditions? This isn't freaking Broadway, it's serving ice cream in suburban Massachusetts.* Mitch informed us that we must go, either individually or in pairs, before the group and find some creative way to express why we want to work for Sweetcone.

I was starting to lose interest in the whole process. *I am not here to be the lead in "Rent." All I'm going to do is serve ice cream.*

This was the first real job I had ever applied for, and I began to wonder if all job interviews were this intense. I decided to not say anything sarcastic, and to just focus on getting the job.

First up was a girl who sang a beautiful song and threw in the word ice cream here and there. Two girls performed a skit, and one guy made up a clever rap about being a server. I was already red with embarrassment as I watched Mitch's eyes move down the line and get closer and closer to Kristine and I. Kristine whispered to me that we should do a cheerleading cheer that we were familiar with, and substitute the word "Sweetcone" for "panthers," our high school mascot.

We entered the middle of the circle, did the simple cheer and the dance moves that went along with it, and ended with a back handspring just for show. At the end of this I was even redder than when I started, but I was thrilled the tryout was over. After everyone completed their audition, Mitch led all of us in one of those roaring rounds of applause that I imagined they did at the end of an AA meeting. Mitch told us that they would be calling us in a week, and thanked us all for coming.

A week went by and neither Kristine nor I had received a phone call. My Dad told me to call Mitch for a follow up. He also mentioned how important a first job is for personal development, learning to deal with people, and understanding how hard I must work to earn money. Then he casually added, "And it won't be a big deal if you bring me home a big bowl of ice cream each time you work."

"I don't know about that," I responded. "The owner never said anything about giving out free ice cream to family members. I'm not even sure I can have any."

"Well I think it's customary. Don't be such a worrywart.

Anyway, give him a call about the job, but don't bring up the bowl of ice cream for Dear Old Dad. And if you don't get the job you can be my assistant in helping me with the yard work. I'll find all sorts of interesting things for you to do, like rototilling the garden and managing the compost pile."

I immediately made the telephone call.

"This is Mitch at Sweetcone, how may I help you?"

"Hi Mitch, this is Kristin Tougias. I auditioned about a week ago and was just wondering when I could expect to hear back about the job?"

"Ah yes Kristin, how are ya? Yeah we've been really busy here at the store trying to get things together for the grand opening..." his voice trailed off as I stared out my bedroom window to watch two kids rollerblading. He went on and on about the store and how hectic his week has been, and I interjected with some "mmmms" and "ahhhs" every few seconds. "Someone will definitely be letting you know by Friday," he promised in his overly energetic voice.

"Great, I look forward to hearing from them! Thank you!" I said in my most cheerful tone and hung up the phone.

The call came on Thursday. Not only did I get the job, but my soon-to-be manager Marsha informed me that I was one of the "five outstanding applicants" selected to train in advance, before any of the other new hires. "Wow," I said excitedly. "Thank you!"

She went on, "Now you and the four other girls we selected will be training the rest of the group. You guys will be kind of like Assistant Managers. And you will be training at our other store until the new store is ready." Her tone was very matter-of-fact, but friendly nonetheless. I was excited to tell my parents about this. *Assistant Manager! Next stop, CEO!* I guess having an audition worked out in my favor, and I couldn't wait to see what the working world was all about.

Training started the following Monday. Kristine got the job too, but to my disappointment wasn't one of the five hired for early training. I drove to the other store where Marsha had said to meet her at 3:30 p.m. Two other girls were already there when I arrived. They were both sophomores at the neighboring high school, and both very nice. Next to arrive was a laid back but outgoing girl named Molly who I liked instantly. We bonded over our shared disdain for the tryout process, which Molly also found to be ridiculous and unnecessary. "It should be interesting having Big Marsha as our manager," she remarked. *Interesting indeed.* From that moment on, Marsha would always be known as "Big Marsha" among all of us.

A few minutes later the final girl arrived who told us to call her "Yam." As we all stood around making small talk, a beat-up, off-white jeep came zipping around the corner of the clothing store next door, flew over a speed bump so fast that all four wheels lifted off the ground, and pulled up in front of us. We all stared in silence as Marsha, our new manager, lumbered out, completely out of breath.

"Hey guys," she said wearily as she walked towards us. I noticed she had on the same clothes as the first day I met her: loose black pants, black shoes, and what can only be described as a "flesh-colored" collared shirt, practically identical to her skin shade, making her appear bare-chested. She wore this outfit daily during my entire tenure at Sweetcone.

Marsha started shaking hands with us, but the girl named Yam hesitated a second, as if considering the odds that once her hand was in Marsha's clutches she might be pulled in tight and eaten like a snack.

"Okay," said Marsha, "only two of you can go with me since I've got a bunch of junk in the back, and three of you will have to go in another car. Anyone willing to drive?"

"I will," Molly said. Two of the girls quickly said they'd join Molly, leaving Yam and me to go with Marsha. I reluctantly took the front seat on the passenger side next to Marsha as Yam bolted to the back. The car was filled with clutter, and for a brief moment I thought Marsha and my Dad must have hatched from the same alien egg. Marsha wedged herself behind the wheel then fired up the engine, and we peeled out of the shopping plaza as if in a "The Fast and the Furious" sequel.

"I apologize in advance for my crazy driving," she said. "I tend to go a little fast."

The apology was by no means in advance—I was already gripping the dashboard the way I would on a roller coaster while Big Marsha pulled onto the three lane highway and crossed into the fast lane in a flash, without ever glancing over her shoulder. "Idiot," she muttered as she swerved right to speed up and pass an older woman in a small grey car. I glanced in the rear view mirror and saw Molly struggling to keep up with the speed and lane switching in her green Jetta. It was hopeless. Marsha was flying, and I looked at the speedometer to see that we were going 92 mph. *Is this real? Are we ice cream scooping trainees or convicted felons involved in a high speed care chase?*

"Ah f**k you," Marsha croaked as she nearly clipped the front of another car by aggressively switching into the right lane again.

"So you guys excited about Sweetcone?" Big Marsha asked, shifting her angry tone to one of total composure in a flash, as if Yam and I could even think while our lives were endangered by her reckless lane crossing.

"Uh huh," I said, my mouth agape as we sped past car after car. I stared at their passengers with the same alarmed facial expression of a kidnapped child signaling they're in grave danger, nearly mouthing the words "help me...."

After fifteen minutes of driving like we were on America's Most Wanted and racing for the Mexican border, we finally reached our exit and then the store. The other girls didn't pull into the parking lot until several minutes later, and one of them gave me a nasty look as if I were the one who floored Marsha's car and left them in the dust.

We all trudged into the store, passing a few customers before heading behind the counter where two teens were working, then into a large back room where a girl with headphones and butt-length hair was busy making cakes. Marsha handed us all a huge packet that said Sweetcone: Employee Training Manual. It had to be at least 50 pages long. As I flipped through the thick manual and waited for Marsha to gather our aprons and hats, I glanced at recipes, exercises, and extensive instructions for operating machinery, mixing flavors, cleaning equipment, and handling customers all scattered amongst photos of people fake smiling and scooping ice cream. When I looked back up, Jasper was before us, exposing his pearl white teeth as he spoke. "Congratulations everyone, and welcome aboard! Today I'll be going over some scenarios with you."

After some employee-customer reenactments performed by Jasper and Big Marsha, all of us practiced responding to different hypothetical situations. I found it hard to keep a straight face as Marsha pretended to be a pretentious woman displeased with her ice cream. After what felt like hours of these tedious drills, Marsha set up a station for us to weigh scoops of ice cream. There were four main sizes, ranging from kiddie to large. With metal scoops, we had to estimate the amount of ice cream to match the size requested. My ball of vanilla was far larger than it should have been as I put it into the plastic container on the scale. "We're going to lose money with this inaccuracy," Marsha snapped, and I could feel her getting frustrated with me when I unintentionally did it a second time.

On my third try my wrist was aching from the arduous pulling effort and the scoop slipped out of my hand, falling back into the bucket of hard ice cream. Marsha pushed me aside, grabbed the scoop and effortlessly pulled up a perfect sphere of ice cream. "That's how it's done," she pronounced, glaring at me.

"Easy for her to do," Molly whispered to me as Marsha walked away. "She's had countless hours scooping it directly into her mouth." I snorted and quickly put my hand to my mouth as Marsha whipped around and stared at Molly and I with distrusting eyes.

I felt vindicated when none of the other girls could accurately eyeball the ice cream's exact weight according to its spoken size. Once we finished that exercise, Jasper put in a video on the computer for us to watch about how to operate the machine that produces the ice cream. The actor going through the motions looked bored to tears. It could have easily been mistaken for a documentary titled "How to Make Others Think You Live a Meaningless, Miserable Life."

At about 5:45 p.m. we finished the first day of training, and I couldn't wait to go home. "One last thing," said Marsha, "Your homework is to memorize the steps in operating the machinery, memorize two of our special ice cream creations, and read the first twenty pages of the manual."

Homework! I signed up to be an ice cream server, not enroll in the Academy of Ice Cream Science. My fellow trainees and I exchanged panicked glances, but nobody spoke up. Perhaps because Marsha stood with her hands on her hips, blocking the door to the parking lot. Finally someone said, "okay."

Marsha shuffled away from the doorway, and with her back to us said, "Dismissed."

Over dinner that night I told my parents about Marsha's crazy driving, and all the procedures, mixtures, specials and responses to customers I had to memorize. I felt a little overwhelmed and was looking for a bit of empathy.

"Wow," my Dad said. "Seems like a good fit. Listen, you probably didn't get a chance to sneak me out any ice cream on your first day, but give it a shot tomorrow."

* * *

The next four days of training that week were made more wearisome by the unpredictability of Marsha's mood swings, which came and went like the ebb and flow of hungry customers. Often when one of us trainees paused to ask a question, Marsha would respond with, "just serve the f'in ice cream!" One hour she was pleasant and the next she would be incredibly crude and insulting, for no apparent reason. But by the third day I began to notice a pattern—whenever Big M's mood took a downturn, all she needed was a scoop of vanilla ice cream flooded in caramel as a pick-me-up. She requested several of these throughout the day, and I nearly gagged whenever it was my turn to deliver the scoop of vanilla drowned in a cup of caramel over to her while trying not to let it spill over the edges. She would slurp it down and within fifteen minutes she seemed both energized yet more patient. It was clear she had some kind of addiction to sugar, just as powerful as the drug addicts featured in our health class videos. And I was literally feeding her addiction, but the alternative was working alongside a bipolar beast who used the "F word" every other minute, so I opted to be her "dealer."

I took my responsibilities as one of the first hires seriously, especially after Big M referred to all of us as the A Team. I liked the level of responsibility that came with being a member of the A Team and memorized all the special creations she asked me to.

It was odd having to train other people my age—among them being Kristine, who found it hard to keep a straight face as I tried to professionally instruct her on how to make the ice cream. In the week that I trained the other servers (ninety-five percent of them being girls), three people asked me how old I was. I was astonished when they shyly confessed that I looked 22. *Wow. Am I really starting to look older than my age?* I thought. *Maybe this job is already giving me fine lines?* I tried the rest of that afternoon to relax my face and smile more.

* * *

After three weeks of training, assembling and organizing the store, the opening day was finally here. And it was ab-so-lute chaos. Molly and I were selected to be the two Assistant Managers on duty that day, and we couldn't seem to do anything right. The peers we trained forgot everything we taught them. We ran out of chocolate ice cream in the first hour, the girl on waffle cone-making duty couldn't produce fast enough to meet the demand of our hungry customers, and our newest hire burst into tears when a customer spoke sharply to her about the ice cream being overpriced. Metal scoops were dropped left and right, hands were racing to grab the last Oreo in the jar before it had to be replaced, and occasionally a scoop of ice cream would fall off a customer's cone and splatter onto the floor just as we handed it to them. I ran over to Marsha to ask her where the backup supply of chocolate ice cream was kept, but before I could even finish the question she cut me off by barking, "Don't worry about that, just serve the f**king ice cream!"

Whatever illusions I had that I would "manage" the crew disappeared as I was ordered to join the staff behind the counter and slave away for irritated parents and moaning kids. It was a job that I hated immediately. I felt like I was scooping cement rather than ice cream, and I was positive I could feel myself getting carpel tunnel. And this was only the first hour.

Big M was trudging around like a pissed-off Santa Claus ready to clock one of his slower elves. The line of customers extended out the door and along the sidewalk of the plaza. Long before closing time we ran out of vanilla and strawberry ice cream in addition to the chocolate, and Marsha announced the news to the line of people. The crowd booed, complaining that they had waited in line for nothing. *What have I gotten myself into,* I wondered. *Is this what I have to look forward to after college when I'm out in the working world?* It was then, and only then, that I contemplated staying in school forever.

The next day when I came in for work, Big M called the staff together and warned us that if anyone, ever, for any reason, touched one of her cans of Pepsi in the twelve pack she kept in the walk-in fridge (which she replenished daily), we would be fired, and that she would give us terrible recommendations for any other job. "And I'll kick your ass for good measure," she added with just the slightest twinge of a grin so as to let you know she was kidding. Or *might* be. It was clear the pressure of running two stores was sending Marsha into a tailspin, and she might take one of us down with her.

The next three weeks were like this—listening to Big M rant about petty crap, laboring away behind the counter to a crowd that never dwindled or seemed satisfied, feeling deflated whenever a customer received a bunch of change back but chose to only put a dime in the tip jar. While it certainly wasn't for us, the store must have been a gold mine for Mitch and Marsha, because even as we tried to lock the doors at 11 p.m., eager ice cream eaters were still filtering in after dinner or the movies. It was the perfect set up for them, and the worst possible scenario for us servers making minimum wage. Always one to love meeting new people, it was now loathsome after serving others for hours straight, and I laughed at myself for thinking this would be the perfect job.

Closing the store was absolute hell. It never took less than an hour to refill every jar of toppings and clean all the blenders with milkshake spattered on the counter, a zillion scoops, and baking sheets. There were several pieces of machinery to be washed and sanitized. Then there was money to count, floors to sweep and mop, and a walk-in fridge and freezer to be organized. It was agonizing manual labor, and by this time of day Big M was in the worst of moods, and even her ice cream fix did little to make her civil. During the store closing and cleaning we would turn up the radio just to make the passing time more bearable, but Big M would roar, "Guys! Turn the f**king music down!" from the back room where she sat playing solitaire.

The only perk of this job was that every employee was granted a free item to take at the end of their shift. After about the second day of work, I was making myself extra large ice creams to replace the dinners I never had while scooping for hours. *I* had become a sugar addict, and I relied on these ice cream creations to get me through the day. Throughout my shift I would dream up the perfect gluttonous combination of candies and flavors—*chocolate ice cream with Snickers, KitKat, caramel and peanut butter*—*no no, mint ice cream with Oreos, Butterfinger, chocolate sauce and rainbow sprinkles.* These thoughts consumed my entire being, and I had become so obsessed with my creamy masterpieces I even started to dream about them. I treated the dreams like premonitions and followed through by making that specific ice cream creation the next day. My favorite take-home item soon became heaps of cake batter ice cream doused with chocolate chips, three Reeses cups, two hunks of cookie dough, drenched in hot fudge. All of us would coyly construct our creations and hide them behind the cans of whipped cream we kept in the mini fridge out front whenever Big Marsha was in the back room.

Apparently Mitch, the franchise owner and boss of Big M, caught onto this, since I was just one of numerous starving employees making a five course meal at the end of their shift. One night, he marched in right at closing time, his usually phony upbeat demeanor replaced with one of real fury. After the last customer had left, Mitch locked the doors and let us have it.

"GUYS!" he yelled. "What is this about people taking more than the allotted item at the end of their shifts? You get one item, ONE FREE ITEM. That is not a freaking pint of ice cream with six different kinds of candy! Okay? This is a f**king privilege, and if it

happens again there will be no free item, do NOT do it again!"
Apparently some amateur had put their feast in the walk-in rather
than the mini fridge which Big M and Mitch never checked.

We were all furious that Mitch would give us grief over a
couple extra scoops of ice cream when he and Big M wouldn't
even allow us our fifteen minute break during our shift and
refused to pay us for the time spent cleaning after the store
closed. I couldn't understand how they got away with all this,
especially the part where we couldn't get our paid break. The
child labor laws poster wasn't even hung in the back room like it
should've been. So from then on each day when I came in to start
my shift, I would take out the rolled poster from the back room
and hang it in plain view, only to find it rolled up and hidden from
me in a new spot the next day. This game of hide-and-seek-the-
labor-laws-poster went on for two weeks before the poster
disappeared altogether.

Us employees got our revenge the only way we knew how—
we ate it. Ate everything we could. I would start every shift by
grabbing a soda, a Reeses and an Oreo before putting on my visor
and apron. And at the end of our shifts everyone went right on
making their enormous sundaes. There was just one problem with
this strategy. I was on my way to looking like Marsha. I noticed
that some of my pants wouldn't button, and I would inspect the
skin beneath my chin for minutes at a time during bathroom
breaks, convinced a double chin was forming. *If I keep this up I'm
going to start wearing flesh colored shirts, and drive on a sugar-
induced high at 90 miles per hour.* So I tried to cut back on my
consumption, giving up the only perk this miserable job had to
offer so I wouldn't suffer a heart attack by thirty. My goal now was
simply to hang onto the job until the end of July, rationalizing that

was a reasonable amount of my summer to give up.

As the summer crawled on, Marsha started leaving the store for increasingly longer periods of time to go help out at the other store she previously had managed. We all knew she liked those kids better, but that store was on a remote road and not in a buzzing shopping plaza, which meant fewer customers and higher sanity levels.

The first day Big M left, Molly pulled me into the back room while the others were serving ice cream. "Come on," she whispered. I knew she was up to no good as she led me into the walk-in fridge and let the door shut behind us. She took out two plastic cups, placed them on a shelf and poured milk to the rim in each. She then walked to another shelf housing boxes of Oreos. Molly reached into an already opened box and emerged with a handful of Oreos to dip into our milk. No one would have questioned our whereabouts because we were the assistant managers on duty, which required being in the back room to man the phone and take care of dishes, schedule changes, etc. We stood there in that walk-in fridge, shivering and manically dunking Oreo after Oreo in our cups of milk faster than we could swallow them, pausing only to let out bursts of low, evil laughter.

When the milk was gone, I went across the fridge to get a Reeses from the backup jar and Molly followed. I paused at the jar, frozen not by the chilly temperature but by what stood eye-level on the shelf before me. There it was, next to the jar of Reeses, beckoning us—taunting us. The Forbidden Fruit.

Big M's beloved twelve-pack carton of Pepsi.

After a long moment's pause, Molly, in a mischievous voice said, "Let's take one."

"What if we get caught?" I asked now in a frightened state.

"We won't," she answered confidently, "There's no way she counts."

I turned my gaze away from Molly and back toward the five remaining cans in the twelve-pack and hoped Molly was right. Big M had probably had her Pepsi fix today, since it was only 5:30 p.m. and seven cans had been drunk. I reached my hand into the box and pulled out a glistening can, cold as ice, appetizing as ever. A shot of adrenaline spiked through my body as I slid a shaking finger underneath the frosty aluminum tab. I hesitated for a moment, feeling as though the world as I knew it might change the second I opened that can. There was no going back. I imagined Big M treating the canned Pepsis as her babies, all living in this protective cardboard box. If she discovered one had been abducted, she'd send out an AMBER alert for the missing Pepsi, and hunt down the kidnapper no matter how cold the trail.

"Open it," whispered Molly. "You can do it."

I felt like I was Eve and Molly the serpent in the biblical tale. I took a deep breath and pulled the tab ever so slowly. The can cracked and hissed carbonation like a venomous snake. I passed the Pepsi to Molly to do the honors. She inhaled a deep breath and took one gentle sip. I stood there wide-eyed, watching her every move, waiting for something to happen. She swallowed, then looked up at me, eyes ablaze, and let out a sinister laugh before passing the can back to me. I had goosebumps all over my body as the two of us stood in the chilly fridge, swapping the Pepsi back and forth, giggling and sipping until the can went dry. Later, Molly put the empty in her car trunk under a blanket to fully dispose of the evidence.

* * *

Big M came back around 7 p.m. She bashed Mitch behind his back for a while, ranting to me about how cheap he was and how she didn't get paid enough as I mixed brownie batter in the back room. Then the store became really crowded, and every employee was sent out in the front to serve ice cream including me. What happened next was a blur.

As I was slicing strawberries and looking around for the whipped cream for an elderly woman's ice cream, I heard Big M's heavy footsteps approaching.

"WHO DA F**K STOLE MAH PEPSI!" she hollered as every customer and employee froze. Squiggly veins protruded from her forehead and the coloration in her face transformed from red to purple with each passing second of silence. When still no one answered, she said it again, even louder this time. "WHO DA F**K STOLE MAH PEPSI?" She was beyond mad—she was unhinged.

I didn't dare to look over at Molly as my heart was pounding and I thought I might pee my pants. Big M was in a rage like I had never seen before, and it is my firm belief that every single person in that store at that moment felt it might be the last moment of his or her life. The only time she came close to being this angry was when people just stopped showing up for work (which was happening more often now), or when someone forgot her cup o'caramel. The room of people remained stunned and speechless, and Big Marsha waited a few seconds before pivoting and storming back into her den.

That was one of the most terrifying moments of my youth. I quickly began to despise Marsha—not for her reaction after the Pepsi incident, but for the entire way she operated the business. I realized that Molly and I probably just made the miserable working atmosphere at Sweetcone even worse by committing the ultimate crime. And while I felt extremely guilty about this, everyone did get a thrill from witnessing Big M become deranged. As we walked to our cars that night, still shaking from the events of the day, Molly and I swore never to tell a soul what we had done.

Big M was on guard now more than ever, and it seemed like she was growing ever more suspicious of me. I began to request being assigned to any duty that didn't involve me serving ice cream or interacting with people—brownie baking, dish washing, shelf organizing, or making the ice cream itself, which involved lifting large sacs of flavored cream weighing the same as a cinderblock and pouring it into a machine that whipped it before being frozen. There was only one consequence to being the employee in the back room versus out front serving customers: it involved much more face time with Big M.

One day, when I was on waffle cone-dipping duty in the back, Marsha received a phone call, and for the first time it wasn't Mitch or a customer inquiring about a custom-made cake. I couldn't quite pinpoint who the mysterious caller was, and after about ten minutes of heated conversation, I figured Big M was so distracted that it was safe to "accidentally" break one of the warm waffle bowls I had just dipped in melted chocolate. I set aside the defective waffle in a separate dish to cunningly eat pieces while I worked. The chocolate covered waffle cone was delicious, and within minutes three more "accidentally" broke.

As I chewed slowly to avoid the crunching sounds, hoping to better eavesdrop on the conversation taking place behind me, it became clear that Big M was having an argument of some sort over money. She fervently denied what seemed to be accusations that she hadn't paid her taxes, and her tone grew more aggravated as she was provoked with more questions. As the conversation drew on, I took fewer and fewer bites to listen more carefully to the legal battle ensuing behind me. She hung up the phone, but the person on the other end called back a minute later. Big M then threatened to file for harassment, and I stood frozen with my back to her, now staring wide eyed at the cabinet in front of me. I gently let down the waffle piece I was munching so that I could really pay attention. Big M had been pacing, and then I heard the squeaky wheels of her rolling leather computer chair shriek as she plopped herself onto the seat. She was huffing and groaning, and I was much too scared to turn around. A moment later I heard the dialing of numbers and a pen nervously tapping on a desk.

"Ah hi, yea, I was just told that they have me on tape lying about paying my taxes?" There was a brief pause, then, "Yea alright...listen—am I going to have two guys in black suits show up at my front door and arrest me? Am I going to jail?" The suspense made me crack another waffle bowl, only this time it really was an accident. The jarring realization had hit me: Marsha was on the phone with the IRS.

I stood frozen and wide eyed with my back to her as silence fell over the back room, and I figured she was counting the minutes she had to flee to Canada before the police would come to the store looking for her. Lost in thought, I dipped a jagged piece of waffle into the chocolate and put it into my mouth.

"Kristin!" Big M screamed, shaking me from my day dream where five cop cars and a helicopter trailed a ramshackle white jeep speeding north at 150 mph.

"Yes?" I responded breathlessly as I whirled around, coughing up a piece of cone still lodged in my throat while using my hand to wipe a dribble of chocolate that had just trickled down my lip.

"I need you back out front," Big M bellowed only a foot from my face, and I watched her eyes narrow on what was most likely my chocolate covered lip. I put down the drenched waffle and headed out front before she had a chance to say anything. But the worry left my mind quickly, for it was she who was in deep trouble. And only I knew it.

* * *

When July came, Molly was promoted to manager and I wasn't. This thrilled me because not only would I not have the responsibilities that she did, but with her now being my friend and overseeing the store, I could do whatever I wanted—which meant I'd never have to serve another ice cream again! I would live in the back room as Molly's personal assistant, eating candy and washing dishes to earn my pay—much of which was being used to buy pants with a larger waist size.

Big M had approached Molly and I a few weeks prior to tell us that we would both be the managers. My parents weren't wild about the idea, since I was already working a lot as it was, but I didn't say anything to Big M for fear of being forced to work behind the counter and scoop ice cream day after day. Instead, I decided on a strategy that might make her reconsider me as "management worthy." And so I began requesting days off at an alarming rate. In the back room was a calendar, and the first ten employees who entered their name as "unavailable" were the people who got that day off. Tough luck if you had a later shift and ten names were already listed on a particular day you needed off.

I learned this the hard way when one day I went to the

calendar to enter my name on an upcoming weekend and saw there were already ten names listed. I went over to Big M sitting at her computer and explained that I was going to New Hampshire that weekend with my Dad. Without ever looking at me she replied, "Sorry, ya had to be one of the first ten on the list," and took a spoonful of caramel to her mouth.

Irritated with this system that had not been previously explained, I whipped around and marched straight towards the calendar. I grabbed a pen started writing my name in a fury on any day with an open "unavailable" slot. Later Big M informed me that because I had requested so many days off, they could not promote me to manager, and Molly got the position. I just smiled at her and nodded my head, pleased with my work.

The first day Big M left and handed Molly the keys to the store was the happiest day of my life. She and I made an unnecessary amount of brownies just so we would have an excuse to eat the batter. At this point six employees had quit without ever giving notice. They just stopped showing up, and the rest of us would have to work twice as hard. When Molly got her promotion to manager she was paid $1.50 more an hour, but couldn't take tips like the rest of us, so in the end she was making no more than she had been before. After she explained this to me, I said, "That doesn't make any sense. You should ask for a raise."

"I know," she responded. "Maybe I will."

The next day after my urging, Molly asked Big M for a pay increase since she wasn't being adequately compensated for her increase in responsibility. Big M went to Mitch, the Oz behind the curtain of the many Sweetcone cons. He told Big M that Molly could partake in tips, so instead of having to spend his own money to pay her what she deserved, he was essentially taking it out of *our* paychecks. I felt really bad for Big M, as she was clearly frustrated and feeling undercompensated herself, and I couldn't blame her for having a miserable attitude working for a cheat like him.

In mid-July I heard a rumor that Big M was getting engaged. *Wow,* I muttered to myself. *Never saw that coming.* I was completely unaware that she was even dating anyone. One day when I was organizing a new shipment of supplies in the back, I decided to ask Big M about the surprising news. "So I hear you're getting engaged!" I said cheerfully as I picked up a box containing what had to be a thousand butterfingers. "Yep, I am," she said flatly. I waited for her to say more, but she went on typing an email.

"Congratulations!" I said after the lack of elaboration. "Who's the lucky guy?"

"His name's Randy," she said shortly. I didn't push the questioning any further, but my imagination ran wild. I pictured Randy to be a quirky computer technician, but not large like Marsha. I envisioned him frail and tiny, creating one of those fascinating couples who resemble polar opposites. I later learned Big M would be absent the next two weeks from work, and when I asked if she was going on a vacation with him, she said, "Ah, nope, nope we're ah, we're going to get the engagement ring in Texas." This sounded odd to me, since I had never heard of anyone going halfway across the country to get a wedding ring, but then again everything she did—like lying to the IRS—was odd.

Business in July skyrocketed, so to assist Marsha and Molly with the store Mitch brought in a reinforcement from our sister store. Matt and was a senior in high school, fairly good looking, and knew everything about Sweetcone. Within three minutes of working with him we all learned that he had perfect SAT scores, was accepted to Harvard but was going to Dartmouth, and was a total jerk. Matt was definitely the kind of guy who thought his book smarts made him superior, which was an absurd notion, because I knew that if he really was as smart as he claimed, the last place he'd be working was at Sweetcone.

When I went in the back to assume my standard position of waffle cone dipper or dish washer, he looked at me like I was insane and snapped, "We need you out front!" I felt myself getting dizzy as the shock and sheer terror hit me like a bullet. It had been so long since I had served ice cream that the thought of slaving away at the counter to a line of endless customers made me want to faint.

Once behind the counter I blanked on the ingredients for half of the ice creams and shuffled around like a blind bear, knocking things over and causing destruction at every turn. It was utterly miserable, and the next two weeks were more of the same. Matt's micro-managing was so unbearable and oppressive I actually began to miss Big M and her twelve packs of Pepsi.

One night after laboring for hours on a busy Friday, I went into the back room in desperate need of water. I was feeling dehydrated, not to mention in physical discomfort by what I could only assume was carpal tunnel. I stepped into the back room and found pompous Matt, sitting in Big M's leather chair, flirting with two other girls I worked with who were a year older than I. They were all sitting around talking and laughing with milkshakes in their hands. Something at Matt's feet caught my eye, and sure enough there was an empty bottle of Bacardi Rum underneath the desk. I continued toward the fridge to fetch my water and considered for a moment what would happen if I told Mitch, but I felt it best to let a bunch of drunks run his store.

I never thought I'd say this, but Marsha's return from her Texas hiatus was the second happiest day of my life. It meant Matt would go back to his store and I'd go back to my happy place working alongside Marsha in the back room. I was in such high spirits the day of her homecoming that I had a large cup of caramel waiting for her as a welcome back gift.

But Big M's glorious return was short-lived. I had just individually unwrapped thirty Snickers bars and was carefully stacking them in a jar out front when she came marching out of the back room. "I need to see half of you in the back right now!" she demanded. I complied and went back with three of my other peers. "Who the f**k spilt the mango juice?" she challenged while pointing a finger to the open walk-in refrigerator. On the back shelf was a carton of mango juice we used for smoothies laying on its side, its contents spilt on the shelf and onto the floor. We stood silently, as if at a wake.

"WHO THE F**K SPILT THE MANGO JUICE?" she bellowed louder. When no one answered she began questioning each of us. But her methods of interrogation were far too intimidating, and so as with the Pepsi incident, Big M never found out who the culprit was. But this time it really wasn't me.

* * *

August was just around the corner, and Molly and I especially despised our jobs because we were never given our fifteen minute break, which meant no time for lunch or dinner. I would leave just before midnight in a ravenous state and eat my huge cake batter ice cream with chocolate sauce, Reeses, cookie dough and Oreo during my ride home with my Mom or Dad, whose passenger seat was slowly becoming a smorgasbord of all my ice cream creations. I also had to unsnap my pants to sit comfortably as my dairy-drenched belly resumed its outward march.

I continued to start my shift by putting my name under every open day I could find in August. Marsha called me from the back room when I was sweeping the floor one night. I put down the broom and headed toward her desk.

She swiveled around in her chair and began to squint curiously at me, the way she did after I overheard the IRS call. I stood before her smiling nervously, waiting for her to speak. Finally she broke the tense silence.

"Why the hell did you take off thirty days in August?"

"What?" I replied scrunching my eyebrows together in confusion.

"Your name is down for thirty days in August. Does this mean you quit?"

After about a ten second pause of us staring and squinting at each other, I responded calmly by lifting my chin and firmly declaring, "I supposed it does."

Inside, I was riveted at the word "quit", and apparently Big M was too. When her mouth dropped in disbelief and her chin hung loose, I knew she was truly stunned. But instead of unleashing a slew of F-words as I had anticipated, Big M closed her mouth and gave me a single nod, as if to really acknowledge me for the first time before swiveling back around in her chair.

* * *

A few weeks after I quit, Molly informed me that Mitch and his wife had gotten divorced, and she thought something else was up when Mitch told her to order fewer supplies. Shortly thereafter, Molly told me that calls began to flood in from companies looking for Mitch claiming he hadn't paid the bills and landlords started showing up asking for rent. In September Mitch filed for bankruptcy and the store was seized. Molly said they never saw or heard from Mitch again.

That summer I learned so much about life, hard labor, and my fat potential. Apparently Big M learned some things too, like how to evade the IRS and fake a wedding, because a week into August I found out that Randy never really existed, and Marsha had never been engaged. That trip to Texas was just a ploy to line up a new job, and perhaps a new identity. I guess I wasn't the only one dying to get out.

As for me, I had gained ten pounds and missed the summer's best parties because I was working so many hours. And while it may have sounded like a failure of a summer on the surface, I knew different. I had stood up to an intimidating boss, witnessed first hand how not to run a business and treat your employees, experienced the thrill of breaking a rule with the Pepsi incident, and I made a lifelong friend in Molly. I wasn't sure how my overall experience there would make me a better person, but it did make me grateful for every single job I would come to hold in the future.

* * *

A Dad's View

I had no idea what was going on at Sweetcone or how difficult Kristin's job was. But even learning about it after the fact, I'm glad she had the experience. When I was a teen I worked every summer job imaginable, from janitor to bag-boy to baker. I would not trade that real world experience for anything, and someday I'll bet Kristin feels the same. Too many kids today go through their middle and high school years without working, and I think they're missing out on how to adapt to different situations and people from all walks of life.

The one thing I will remember about Kristin's Sweetcone experience is the day that employees' family members were invited to the grand opening for a free ice cream cone. I barged into the store belting out my best Julie Andrews, singing, "The hills are alive with the sound of music" to get Kristin's attention. It worked. Kristin rushed to the front of the store and shot me an evil look.

"What?" I said, "would you prefer I did something more modern like the Beatles?"

I knew she was cringing, and I could see her friend Kristine standing in the background suppressing a laugh.

"Ok, ok, I'll shut up," I said. "Anyways, congratulations on your first job!" Then I introduced myself to the other kids working while Kristin went behind the counter to get my ice cream cone.

Five minutes later, she surprised me. She exceeded the call of duty, and instead of an ice cream cone she handed me a super-sized sundae. I was so proud of her. A chip off the old block if ever there was one. She might act like I drive her nuts, and maybe I do, but that gesture meant so much to me.

When I was finished with the sundae, I gave Kristin a hug and whispered, "You don't suppose you could make me another, but this time with pieces of Snickers in it..."

CHAPTER 6

MY FREE WEEKEND AT THE OUTHOUSE

After inadvertently quitting my job by taking off 30 days in August, I used the last remaining weekend of the summer to take another trip with my Dad, this time to his cabin in Vermont.

This ramshackle old A-frame structure—his pride and joy—identically mirrored his quirky and eccentric nature. When my father was a teenager he dreamed of living like a mountain man. While other young men had their sights and paychecks aimed on sporty new cars, my father was saving every dime to buy his own cabin. He was able to purchase the property by age 22 and began spending summer weekends there. It was at this remote hilltop, where the cabin stood like a sentinel overlooking a large pond below, that my Dad seemed most happy.

He recently told me that he and my Mom first took me there when I was just five months old, and that he put me in a baby backpack and we went fishing on the Lamoille River. "You brought me good luck," he said. "We must have waded down the river for a half a mile, casting the whole time, but we eventually caught a nice fat rainbow trout." He showed me a picture my Mom took of that trip where I'm fast asleep in the backpack, my head resting against his neck. My Dad has his fishing waders on, holding his rod in one hand the trout in the other. He's got a smile from ear to ear.

I vaguely recall snatches of impressions from some of the "backpack outings" when I was a bit older. It was like being carried through a movie of vivid changing colors, from the blue water of the mountain brooks rushing by to the dazzling yellows and reds of the fall foliage. In many ways these outings were like going horseback riding—I was up high, my Dad was my sure-footed steed, and we traveled through beautiful countryside. Better still, this horse could talk. He would point out trees and plants to me, identifying them as we went along. He then began quizzing me on each of our hikes, and by the age of three I could identify most all species of trees in the New England terrain we explored together.

My first detailed memories of the cabin trace back to about age five or six after I had graduated from the backpack now used by Brian during his toddler years. Our family would swim in the pond, go for short hikes or sit outside the cabin toasting hotdogs and marshmallows by campfire. At that age everything about the place was new and adventurous from stargazing at night, to catching frogs and fish, to our unsuccessful attempts at answering the hoot of barred owls in the evening.

It wasn't until I was ten or eleven years old that I appreciated just how different the cabin was from our home in suburban Massachusetts. Even driving to the cabin was a real adventure. Once we exited the highway, the roads got progressively rougher and steeper. First the pavement ended and we traveled on a wide dirt road, but soon the road narrowed and began climbing through a dark forest of hemlock, birch and spruce trees. The bumps and ruts in the road made for slow going as we left civilization behind and passed through little valleys where beavers created broad marshes. By the time we reached the pond that the cabin was perched above, the road was not much more than a lane with a bit of grass growing from the middle. Brian and

I braced ourselves for the best part of the ride—the "driveway"—
a quarter-mile path hacked into the woods that only an intrepid
driver with a four wheel drive vehicle would venture on.
Passengers bounced from side to side while my Dad negotiated
washouts, boulders, and two hairpin turns. First time visitors to
the cabin usually began to worry just what they had gotten
themselves into at this point. The car moaned and creaked as my
Dad forced the old Subaru to climb the hill at a speed that made
everyone uneasy.

"I've got to keep momentum," he once explained. "One time I
went up the hill too slow and the wheels started spinning in a wet
spot and we slid off the driveway and into a rut. A farmer had to
come with a tractor and chains to pull me out. It took all day."

The driveway suddenly ended at a small clearing where the
cabin commanded a sweeping view of the mountains to the north
and the pond two hundred feet down the ridge. The scene from
the cabin deck was worth the trip—the cabin itself, well, not so
much. Rustic is too kind a word. The first floor was one big room
filled by a table and chairs, a lumpy and tattered old couch, and
four mattresses piled in a corner. A tiny window graced the back
of the room and an even smaller one was in the front next to a
sink. This sink fooled many a visitor, as the cabin had no running
water. And that meant no bathroom and no shower.

"You don't need either," my Dad has repeatedly pointed out.
"Mankind has been using outhouses or a private spot in the woods
for thousands of years. And who needs a shower when we have
the pond." What he failed to mention was that showers have hot
water while the pond was ice cold, and modern bathrooms do not
have a plethora of critters living inside of them.

There was a second floor to the cabin, but no one dared pull down the hanging stairs to climb up. When I was a kid and asked if I could go up there, my Dad answered, "I haven't been up there in a couple years. The last time I did I was greeted by a raccoon. Probably best to just let sleeping dogs or raccoons lie." He went on to explain that the second floor was one big unfinished room. "There are cracks in the rear wall that bats can fit through to roost up there during the daytime. More like a cave than anything else." Thus we gave the bats their space while they respected ours.

The cabin did have one thing I looked forward to no matter what my age: the guest books. These guest books were like time capsules, where twenty-something year old versions of my Dad and decades of visitors recorded their experiences. Upon entering my teenager years, the first thing I did after arriving was locate guest books of years past and read my entries, beginning from when they were just scribbles then moving to a few sentences with pictures. Seeing my handwriting and the depth of my stories transform year over year fascinated me, and it always amazed me how different my current life was from when I recorded those past visits.

For being one of the most tranquil spots on earth, the cabin saw its fair share of dramatic moments. There was a blowout fight between Brian and I when we were little which resulted in him ripping the tusks off my beloved childhood stuffed animal "Walrus," sending me into mania. A few years later, Brian was eating from a jar of mixed nuts one night when he had a life-threatening allergic reaction. And there was the time my parents woke up with a dead mouse in the bed with them.

While I loved going to the cabin when I was younger, I wasn't too wild about spending a precious weekend there during my high school years. I was a typical teen in how I viewed such a far off place in the woods, complaining to my Mom how there was nothing to do there and it took me away from my friends. Plus there was the bathroom situation—or complete lack thereof, which would send any teenage girl into hysterics. But I never had the heart to tell my Dad because I knew how much our trips to the cabin meant to him.

* * *

After my short-lived but highly dramatic tenure at Sweetcone, I was looking to get away and clear my head (and maybe some of my arteries) before entering another year of high school. My Dad, Brian and I arrived at the cabin late at night on a Friday. As he parked the ancient Subaru, my Dad pulled out a little flashlight and led us through the screened porch where he unlocked the door. Being so remote, the area is completely silent and enveloped in total darkness. Brian and I followed our Dad inside, guided only by the beam of the light through the pitch black. I was thinking about thumbing through the guestbook when after just taking a step inside the cabin, my Dad screamed, "Ahhhhh!!" Hearing him scream made me scream, and a second later all three of us were screaming in tandem as the flashlight landed on the face of a bear with its mouth open, fangs displayed.

"Run!" Brian shouted.

Just when I thought I was a second away from peeing in my pants, I heard a giggle come from the direction of my Dad. I whipped my head around and caught him trying to suppress the laughter. "I'll save you!" he hollered, taking a step inside the dark cabin rather than out the door.

"There's another one!" he shouted, and he let his flashlight beam rest on a second bear, this one a bit smaller, standing on its hind legs. Then he shined the flashlight back on the head of the bigger one, whose body was behind the lumpy old couch. I looked at its glazed eyes and realized the bear was not alive. It was a taxidermy bear head mounted on a plaque.

"Very funny," I said.

My father reached over by an outdated refrigerator and turned on the room's main light. We could now make out the smaller bear, which too was stuffed.

"Gotcha!" my Dad said laughing.

"Where did you get them?" Brian asked.

"Uncle Bob bought the bear head, and a library gave me the stuffed bear. The librarian said it had been in their attic for years, and that I was the only person she could think of who might want it."

"She was right," Brian replied. "You need to get a life."

"Yeah, yeah," my Dad answered. "You should have seen me driving up here a few weeks ago with that bear strapped into the passenger seat."

Once our breathing stabilized from the bear prank, Brian and I made a campfire after he changed into his aptly-named "cabin shirt"—a plaid button-down of brown, green, and beige hues. We sat by the fire and ate some leftover cold pizza from the night before while my Dad handed each of us a "roasting stick" and a hot dog. Not typically a fan of hotdogs, I found anything we roasted over the open fire at the cabin to be delicious. Although this time there was something different ... something ... alarming about the taste of these hot dogs. After taking a second bite I nearly gagged, and apparently Brian did too as a piece of his hotdog came flying out of his mouth and landed in the grass below. "Ewwww," we both said, grimacing and staring at this thing at the end of our sticks in revulsion. Brian had entered a full-blown gag-fest at this point and I was beginning to worry about him.

"How'd you like those soy dogs?" my Dad asked while dragging an Adirondack chair over to the fire.

"Those were nasty," Brian said, and I could actually hear the nausea in his voice. They were probably a few weeks past their expiration date. So nauseous myself, I didn't dare open my mouth to speak for fear of what might come out.

My Dad just laughed and changed the subject. I could tell he was quite pleased with himself, first trying to trick us into believing there were bears in the cabin, and now with these imposter hotdogs.

Brian and I flung what was left of our soy dogs into the woods. We toasted some marshmallows and told a few stories, then my Dad brought out some popcorn.

"Is it real popcorn?" I asked. I was afraid it might be some kind of kale and broccoli concoction that just looked like popcorn. Luckily it was the real thing.

I was thirsty but exercised incredible restraint by allowing myself no more than a sip of water. My goal was to dehydrate myself as best I could to avoid having to pee in the night, because using the outhouse was downright scary. I had nothing but the support of a tiny, dull flashlight to illuminate the narrow path that led into the dark woods and behind the cabin where the outhouse sat, resembling more of a shack from a low-budget horror movie than a restroom.

The outhouse was essentially a small wooden shed, painted red with a lopsided roof. After opening the door, visitors were greeted by a round white toilet seat which sat in the center of a makeshift wooden bench. A tattered roll of toilet paper suspended by a stick was situated next to the toilet.

The outhouse was built above a very large, deep pit in the ground. I feared bears every time. And so I made it a point never to use it at night.

Sleep came quickly once inside the cabin, and I only woke once when I heard my Dad throw his boot across the room. I sat up with a start but didn't bother to ask what he was doing. I knew he had heard a mouse. I put my head back on the pillow, content to let him battle the mouse if it returned. I wondered what was going on back home. I had that same feeling when I missed Jess's pool party for the North Lake trip a year prior, and I thought of all the things I might be missing against the backdrop of my Dad's futile attempt to catch a mouse.

* * *

Saturday morning after breakfast Brian and I went swimming in the pond. It was a beautiful sunny day, the water felt great and the silence of the woods was soothing. I was lying on the raft with my eyes closed, about to doze when the shriek of a chainsaw startled me, and I knew chainsaw fever had overtaken my Dad as it always did here.

Chainsaw fever is a term I coined to describe my Dad's obsession with clearing the view overlooking the pond and cutting firewood at the cabin. He was flat-out obsessed with using that tool since he bought it just a few years earlier. He transformed whenever he suited up in bright orange chaps and helmet and pulled the cord to make the chainsaw roar.

Brian and I heard the shrill of the saw, picked our heads up from the raft where we had been sunbathing and watched a tree fall in the distance.

"Sometimes I wonder if he's so obsessed that he's actually just sawing a lot of little branches most of the time," I said.

"Yea," Brian answered. "I bet he goes after twigs."

"Showing no mercy. Taking no prisoners," I replied.

Two hours later and covered in sweat and tiny woodchips, my Dad trudged up the hill to the deck where Brian and I had retreated to eat some lunch.

"Don't you think the view looks better?" he asked.

"Oh yea," said Brian sarcastically in between bites of his turkey sandwich, "I can see all the way to Canada."

My Dad didn't seem phased by the comment, nor by the fact that he was covered in debris. Instead he announced, "Alright you two, finish up your sandwiches. We're driving to the river and spearing some suckers!"

* * *

After a ten minute drive and a short hike to a beautiful surging river, we whittled sticks to aid in our attempt to spear what my Dad called "suckers," or large fish known to stay in a pack and dwell in a deep pool of this particular river. They were in the same exact spot every single year, and every single year we labored for hours trying to catch one. The three of us sat on a flat boulder, secured our masks over our faces and dove into the ice cold pool. Sure enough, the sucker pack was in the same spot as years previous. We struggled tirelessly to catch one, swimming to the surface for air then diving back down with our spear sticks in hand. After fifteen minutes of relentless spearing while fighting the strong current, Brian and I gave up and retreated to dry land. But my Dad remained persistent, making failed attempt after failed attempt to send his spear into the side of a fish.

While sitting by the edge of the water, Brian found two smooth round rocks congealed together side by side.

"Wow," my Dad said observing the bizarre rock formation thirty minutes later when he finally emerged from the river. "Those look like boobs."

"Oh wow, you're right!" Brian said animatedly. I rolled my eyes and thought here we go.

But as I looked down at my feet, I noticed another smooth rock in the shape of a perfect four-leaf clover.

"Wait, look at this!" I said excitedly, and held up the rock to them.

"Holy moly, these are incredible!" my Dad exclaimed. "Let's see if we can find more."

This launched the beginning of an all out rock hunt. The three of us spread out and set off to find more of these mystifying rock formations. "I found one!" someone would signal to the others after finding another bizarre rock, no two looking the same.

Just a few minutes into our hunt, things got competitive. It then became a quest of who could outdo the other by finding the latest and greatest rock. Never in my wildest dreams did I see myself spending a summer Saturday as a teenager partaking in a rock competition. My Dad was in his element, scouting the riverbank for rock mutants, squealing as if he'd found a hidden treasure every time he stumbled across one.

We left the river that day with about 30 rocks in various shapes, bragging in the car ride back to the cabin about who had the most uniquely shaped rock.

"The perfect heart rock that I found definitely wins," I said.

"No—my boob rock wins," Brian said.

"No," my Dad interjected defiantly. "My rock that looks like a seal takes the cake."

Brian and I looked at each other in confusion, not having the slightest clue as to which rock he could possibly be talking about.

We drove back to the cabin laughing off the high of that sweet sense of discovery and primal accomplishment. But once we got out of the car and opened the trunk to unload our things, we just stared at the 30 rocks now in our possession. "Wow," my Dad said. "What the heck are we going to do now with all these rocks?"

* * *

Back at the cabin, my Dad cooked us a dinner of Swiss chard, striped bass, and green beans mixed with our leftover home fries from breakfast. Later, Brian and I made a fire for cooking s'mores. My Dad sniped the marshmallow bag from my hands and grabbed not one, not two, but six marshmallows and cooked them all, his frail twig bending the way a rod curves when it hooks a fish. He was acting like one big kid rather than a father, and it was nice to see him so relaxed.

That evening the three of us sat on the deck in silence, staring out at the pond and mountains, and in no time found ourselves embedded in the kind of deep conversation that is only experienced when no phones, TVs, computers or other distractions are available. It had been an amazingly simple day, and not once did I think about the pool parties back home I might be missing. Why was I so hesitant to come? It felt so nice to be far from the stresses of high school and my petty job. The cabin grounded me and cleared my mind. It was the one place where I could be completely at peace with no cares or worries.

"This sure beats serving ice cream, doesn't it Kristin?" my Dad asked.

"You don't even know," I said. "Dad, when you were 22 years old and bought the cabin, did you ever envision you would be sitting here with a son and daughter?"

He laughed before answering. "I probably couldn't think past 30!"

I realized I was probably the same way. Who can think about their life that far down the road? I sat on the deck, mesmerized by the view and the way the three of us were sharing stories and giving one another advice. Wasn't it just yesterday when Brian was in the backpack and I was holding my Dad's hand on a hike around the pond? So much time passes and slips away, yet every trip to the cabin was like turning back the clock, revisiting summer vacations and moments that lay dormant in the mind until solitude and staring at ripples in the pond stirred them back to life.

I stopped worrying about school and my social life and the pressures of being a teen. I focused on that present moment. Only here did that happen, and I was so grateful for the spirit in that 22-year-old Dad of mine who had the foresight to know how much joy this tiny, unassuming cabin would bring to his children and his (brave) visitors for decades to come.

* * *

A Dad's View

I'll admit I can be thick-headed, but I did recognize that my two teenage kids might rather have been hanging out with friends than communing with nature in an outhouse that could collapse at any moment. But there was a method to my madness of putting a bit of pressure on them to come to the cabin. My theory was that if I exposed them to some of the fun things in the great outdoors while they were still young, they might just return to these outdoor activities when they are older and under less peer pressure to hang with the herd.

I was proud of the fact that both Kristin and Brian learned how to catch trout in a small mountain stream, prepare the fish for dinner, build a fire when the woods are damp, snorkel and kayak down fast flowing rivers, and be comfortable deep in the woods at night. These may not be the skills necessary for college or to land a job, but maybe they are just as important. I hoped they gave the kids a feeling of self-reliance and accomplishment, and I was certain they enjoyed trying new things. Keeping carefree, old fashioned fun in a teenager's life is not just important, it's essential. We're all just passing through... and my kids have heard me say that. And sometimes I even admonish myself by saying, "Not so serious in this brief life."

* * *

While at the cabin I thought of Kristin and Brian going off to college someday and it made me a little sad, knowing my day-to-day contact with them would soon be gone. But that was offset by knowing my wife and I did our best to raise them to be independent, where they will fly on their own without us giving them instructions. I think the cabin helped with that transition. Up on that ridge-top retreat in Vermont, Kristin and Brian learned far more than they realized because much of their experience came from trial and error. Sure, I gave them quick lessons on how to split wood, cast a fishing lure, and find crayfish under rocks, but the most satisfying part of observing them at the cabin was how unstructured their time was. There was no sitting in a classroom and trying to absorb what teachers were saying. There were no organized after-school activities like the softball, basketball, dance, and football. There was no one to impress. Kristin and Brian figured out how to have fun on their own. I watched them do silly dives and flips off the raft in the pond, make torches at night out of birch bark, and create strange concoctions for dinner. Sometimes, when rain showers kept them on the porch, they took a nap or curled up with one of the old books kept at the cabin and read strictly for pleasure.

My elaborate plan to trick and terrorize my kids with the bear head and the standing bear cub was worth the effort, but the simple substitution of a soy dog for a hot dog turned out to be even better. And that's the beauty of the cabin—less is more, and the simple things outshine the complex. Of course when I bought the cabin I did it for selfish reasons, never dreaming that someday I'd have children who might benefit from the experience of a few days in the woods. I purchased the cabin in my 20's so that I'd have a place to escape the rat-race and pretend I was a mountain man. In my 30's the cabin yielded another bonus, providing me a quiet place to write my earlier books, one of which was about my misadventures there, titled *There's A Porcupine In My Outhouse*. And now I'm in my 50's and I'm counting on the cabin to be part of the glue that keeps my kids close to me, even when they are adults and living far away.

CHAPTER 7

A DAD AND GRAD ABROAD

7 years later

With the start of my sophomore year of high school I underwent a complete transformation, and high school life as I knew it began to change for the better. I finally quit dance, my grades were better than ever, I loved my classes, made incredible friends, joined theater, ran for class secretary and won, and had an amazing boyfriend for years. I then attended Providence College where I truly felt I had found my place in life and was becoming the person I always wanted to be. Those horrid teenage years were now behind me, which I'm sure my Dad was beyond thankful for, because as a father-daughter duo we were closer than ever. He no longer embarrassed me with his purple tattered belly shirt or his dirt-smeared sneakers which he would smother in Vaseline to make "waterproof," and I finally stopped caring about his car and learned to just accept and embrace him for exactly who he was— my eccentric, adventurous, loving father.

* * *

As a college graduation gift, my Dad (after some convincing) took me with him to France to interview the main character for his next survival at sea book, *A Storm Too Soon*. We built an itinerary around a few points of interest in France and Italy, renting a car throughout to experience multiple areas. I was 22 years old and had almost no expectations for this trip—my Dad had never been to Europe, so this would all be new to him. I had studied abroad in Italy and traveled to Paris on a weekend during college, but I had never visited the French Riviera where we were headed. I had no idea what the man we were staying with would be like, or how driving a stick shift rental car through two countries would be, or if the GPS I ordered would be accurate on another continent. But what I did know was that having no expectations meant this trip would be full of stories and surprises.

The trouble—my Dad's trouble—started just shortly after we boarded the plane in Boston. We were lucky enough to have seats in the emergency exit row, which gave us a little extra legroom. Just before takeoff he decided to use the lavatory. The seatbelt sign was on, but he didn't notice as he stood and started toward the rear bathroom. A stewardess, standing in the front, began to yell, "Sir! Sir!"

With the jet's engines warming for takeoff, my Dad couldn't hear the stewardess and he continued his march past rows of perplexed and securely fastened passengers. I watched as the stewardess scowled, came over to our row of seats, and parked herself squarely in the aisle. "Are you traveling with that man?" she asked, as I watched him disappear into the rear bathroom. I wanted to say no.

"Yes," I said with some hesitation. "He's my Dad."

"Didn't he hear me calling him?"

"I guess not."

"The seat belt sign is clearly illuminated. Everyone has to stay in their seat just prior to and during takeoff. I'm not sure why he thinks he's above the rules."

"I don't think he saw the seatbelt sign and he couldn't hear you calling him."

"Then he shouldn't be sitting in the emergency row."

"Why not?"

"Because we have rules that you can't sit in these seats if you have a disability."

"What disability?" I asked.

"Well he obviously has a hearing disability, and you just confirmed it by acknowledging he couldn't hear me."

"Well, no...."

"I'm sorry but those are the rules."

About this time my Dad came sauntering back to his seat, which was blocked by the stewardess, and I held my breath. I could feel a confrontation brewing, and I had visions of my Dad being escorted off the plane in handcuffs, never getting beyond Logan Airport, all because he needed to pee.

When he reached our seats he smiled broadly at the stewardess and said, "Can't wait to take off. I've never been to France." I noticed he even had the hint of an English accent in his voice, as if this would make him sound a bit more worldly.

"Sir—did you not hear me calling you back to your seat?"

"Nope, couldn't hear a bloody thing with these engines revving."

"Well, you are going to have to move your seat."

About this time he dropped the English accent.

"What are you talking about?"

"The rules state that no individual with a disability can sit by the emergency exit door."

"What disability?"

"You obviously are hard of hearing, and your daughter just confirmed this."

I waited for the onslaught of some sort of embarrassing public argument, but instead, my Dad shot me a perplexed look, and then turning back to the stewardess, calmly said, "I can hear just fine. But if you want to move my seat to first class I'm not going to argue."

By now everyone sitting in the surrounding rows was staring at the two of them in anticipation of this discussion reaching a climax.

The stewardess looked like she was ready to explode, but she maintained control and slowly—pausing between each word—said, "You will not be in first class."

I shot my Dad a pleading look that I hoped conveyed what I was thinking—*please don't talk back and ruin this trip before it even starts.*

"Ok," he said in a calm voice. "Whatever you say."

I was both flabbergasted and relieved. It seemed the days when my Dad would start an argument with an 85 year old woman in Florida for cutting him off and sniping his beach parking spot were long behind us. I wanted to hug him for showing such restraint, for picking up on my fear, and for letting this moronic misunderstanding pass.

The stewardess, with a smug look on her face, said, "I'll now show you to your new seat."

Having to get one last word in, my Dad responded with, "I'm

sorry, but I couldn't hear you. Could you repeat yourself?"

The stewardess glared at him, started to say something but apparently changed her mind. She wheeled around and spoke to the audience of passengers, each already giving her their full attention due to the current debacle unraveling before them. "Is there anyone who wouldn't mind switching seats with this man?" she asked. When no one responded, she repeated herself, adding, "this seat in the emergency row has more legroom."

A man of large girth then heroically rose to the occasion. "I'll take you up on that offer," he said, running his hand through a mop of black hair that looked like it had been doused in olive oil.

And so, in typical cringe-worthy fashion, our father-daughter trip to foreign land began. An hour later he came down the aisle, as it must have been pee time again. "Dad! Can you get me one of the books out of your bag? I forgot mine."

Not missing a beat he said, "I'm sorry, did you say you want a bagel?" Then he smiled and said, "I'll get it on the way back. You just sit and enjoy your legroom."

* * *

We arrived in Paris at the Charles De Gaulle airport at 6 a.m., and after finding no open seats, found some floor space in a busy terminal to sit and wait for our connecting flight. I had just opened up the book he retrieved for me when all of a sudden my Dad reached into his backpack, pulled out a large tomato and begin eating it like an apple. "Look at this!" he said holding it out to my face. "One of my tomatoes from the garden made it all the way to Paris!"

"Are you feeling alright?" I joked as he bit in again. "Maybe the jet lag is setting in."

"Yup, I should be in great shape tonight," he said sarcastically while taking another bite of the tomato, lost in thought, letting trails of red juice drip down his chin. "Yup. I should be totally incoherent later. By the way, want a Snickers?"

I knew this sounded suspicious, for my Dad rarely purchased anything, *especially* candy bars. He has been known to stash Halloween candy in his closet for years, the hoarding dating back to my childhood trick-or-treating trips from the early 90's. But I was feeling a bit jet lagged myself and my judgment was cloudy. "Sure," I said, and the second I peeled back the wrapper, I knew I had made a mistake. What was probably—some decades ago— once a delicious Snickers was now a completely disintegrated skeleton of a candy bar, and I swear the package's contents turned to dust the second it met open air. "Ew..." I moaned in outrage as some greyish-white crumbles fell onto my lap.

"I'll have it," he said, reaching over and snatching the Snickers from me. I watched in astonishment as he poured the aged bits into his mouth. "You know," he said as he chewed and looked out at the masses of travelers, "the airport is a good place to be when you're homeless. Remember that if you are someday." Apparently having just graduated *summa cum laude* did nothing in the way of assuring him I'd secure a different fate.

My Dad had insisted we bring only carry-on luggage, and not owning a small enough suitcase myself, I had to borrow one he used to transport books, which he normally kept in my arch nemesis, the Subaru. Even the suitcase was decaying, held together only by the graces of three resolute pieces of duct tape.

Was everything he owned in shambles?

It took us a full hour to retrieve our rental car, and witnessing my Dad's attempt to communicate with a French man was priceless. I could have helped, but thought it better to reap the comedic benefits of the situation at his expense and let him acclimate to being a foreigner on his own. The language barrier between he and the car rental man was as thick as it gets and involved a lot of head shaking, pointing and exaggerated body poses. It was how I'd always envisioned an alien and a human meeting for the first time.

When we were finally out on the open road, my Dad became unhinged, howling and honking the horn repeatedly, so amused with himself for driving a stick shift and navigating the car through foreign terrain. We rounded cliff after cliff with no barriers in place to prevent us from soaring over the edge, and I had to hope his manic laughter was in fact due to amusement with his stick driving skills versus jet lag delirium and lunacy.

The survivor and protagonist featured in my Dad's next book was named Jean-Pierre, or "JP," who is a dual citizen of the U.S and France and speaks both languages. JP met us in a remote village composed of stone houses, winding roads and narrow alleys, and after exchanging introductions we followed behind him in our car to his home. With each passing minute the road grew ever more remote, and at every single turn my Dad and I remarked how this one *must* be his driveway. But each time we were wrong as we continued down winding trails of pebbles, debris, and dirt littered with potholes, all of which featured a death turn around a mountain every fifty yards. My Dad's cackling had completely subsided at this point and was replaced with total concentration, which I was thankful for. He now felt our impending mortality at every turn as I did.

Eventually a driveway did emerge which led us to a stone compound. Dating back to the 15th Century, JP explained that he lived on a "hamlet," or a compound consisting of about five houses in close proximity to one another. He and his neighbors made up their own little hamlet community where there are no street addresses or house numbers. The postman just knows the family name in the hamlet.

After a brief tour of the grounds and our guesthouse, which was equipped with two bedrooms, a bathroom and a fully stocked fridge, I sat by a small in-ground pool adjacent to the patio where my Dad and JP were seated at a wooden table, engaged in heated conversation about American versus European politics. Exhaustion swept over me the second I lay down and drowned them out, and I fell into a deep sleep on the flat stones bordering the pool, waking only at the word "wine" an hour later when JP asked me if I'd like a glass. For a moment I thought I was in heaven and must have died soaring off a cliff in the rental car.

JP was friendly, soft-spoken and intelligent. His wife Mayke was a warm, witty woman from Holland, and the four of us talked for hours during our dinner consisting of fish, vegetables, boiled potatoes and more red wine, and for dessert a bowl of fresh fruit. JP told us a story of his large dog mauling a friend of theirs when she came to visit, but noted that this dog had unfortunately died recently. Later when we went back to our room, I was heading to bed and my Dad said, "Thank god that dog is dead. Goodnight."

The next day, we awoke early and had breakfast at a small table on a terrace outside of our room. I had cherry yogurt, a croissant with butter, an orange from a tree in the hamlet, tea, and a huge slice of French cheese. My Dad took his breakfast to go as he roamed around the grounds, scouting the terrain for wild boars which are known to be vicious there. When he returned unscathed, we hopped into JP's car, and I asked him if it was worth seeing other areas of France or perhaps Cannes. "Neither," JP said flatly, and I knew this meant we would not be visiting any other glamorous places in France as I had hoped.

We drove to Saint Tropez where JP kept his boat. And just like the day before, it was nothing short of a miracle that we managed to avoid driving off the road as JP whipped his car around dirt trails like he was in the Indy 500, just barely hugging the edge of staggering cliffs with his wheels. My Dad was in the passenger seat as I sat in the back, and we held on to whatever we could, gripping the inside of the car the same way we would riding a crazed bull. Further fueling our fear was the fact that JP's right arm was dislocated and in a sling, and he drove with his less-coordinated left hand. To make matters more terrifying, it was impossible to see oncoming cars flying down the winding one lane road. When we finally reached the main paved highway, I realized I had been holding my breath for several minutes.

As we approached Saint Tropez, JP stopped at a store to pick up ham and cheese baguettes for lunch while my Dad ordered himself two chocolate croissants as an after-breakfast snack. We then reached the harbor and walked to a quiet little marina with colorful houses and massive white boats. On the boat next to JP's were two French girls around my age with long hair and big sunglasses who were lounging, drinking wine and chatting in French. They looked a lot cooler than I did being a frumpy tourist sporting sneakers and hanging with two old men.

We sailed to an inlet where the mega rich live and each home costs upwards of around $40 million, and suddenly the thousand dollars I had saved in my checking account didn't seem like much. Perhaps I *would* be homeless after all. But regardless of feeling like a peasant in Saint Tropez, the September day was gorgeous, and as it wore on more boats anchored in the inlet. Families, friends and couples spent the day on their sailboat or yacht to eat, chat, swim and sun. JP and my Dad discussed JP's life story for the book as I simultaneously listened and people-watched.

At 5 p.m. we headed back to the marina and passed a large yacht with an extremely wealthy and attractive young couple making out, drinking wine and blasting techno music. JP and my Dad were disgusted as JP remarked he thought a scene like that was "an outrage," so it was a good thing I didn't tell them that would have been my ideal day at sea.

On the way home JP bought several bottles of wine, and I thought it the second miracle of the day that they didn't all burst on the terrifyingly violent ride back. While my Dad interviewed JP after dinner, his wife Mayke and I stood on the patio to gaze at the stars, which were infinitely more visible here than anywhere I had been. We shared our fascination for the universe and for the unknown at large. "What's it all mean?" she would say. I kept staring and wondered the same.

The next day we went to Grimaud, an old and beautiful village built into a steep hill supporting the ruins of a castle. We climbed curving steps toward the ruins of an ancient castle tower, passing brightly colored flowers and vines flowing from rooftops. Later, while JP had a doctor's appointment, my Dad and I found a small cafe and ordered *deux café au lait* and *deux crêpes au chocolat*. After the sugar-loaded breakfast, JP took us to a restaurant for a three-course lunch of salad, fish and scallop risotto, followed by cake and wine. That evening for dinner he made herring in two sauces, one garlic based and one mustard based, with tomato, fresh bread, potatoes, avocados with olive oil and honey mixed together in the hollowed pit, and for dessert three types of cheese. It was a day that revolved entirely around food, and I seriously contemplated moving myself to France to make this an acceptable lifestyle.

* * *

When it was time to journey onward to Italy, we said a heartfelt thank you and goodbye to Mayke and JP. They had been beyond hospitable, and the four of us grew quite close during our four days at their hamlet tucked away in the hillside of La Garde-Freinet. We then set off for the six hour drive to Carasco in the Liguria region of Italy. While it was only day four of the trip, the rental car was already beginning to smell like my Dad's Subaru back home. And it was starting to resemble it too—maps sprawled out everywhere, dirt-smeared water bottles rolling back and forth across the floor, food wrappers on the back seat. There were faint scratches along the doors now, and the front license plate was hanging off after being clipped during a mountain turn cut too close. The leftover French cheese we took from JP's guesthouse had sat in the car too long and began sweating like a pig in heat, its juices seeping out and leaking onto the back seat. The whole car was a sweltering, stinking cheese mobile, and I was its prisoner for six hours.

When we crossed the border of France into Italy we decided to take a break at a cafe in a piazza, sitting outdoors together with two cappuccinos while we people-watched for a half an hour, sharing laughs over the many interesting Italian outfits. But they stared at us as much as we stared at them. My Dad was one to talk, wearing faded jean shorts he likely bought sometime in the 8th grade, a hat as stiff as stale bread, a green puke-colored collared shirt, a black backpack from god knows where, and his dirt-smeared gardening sneakers with tethered laces.

That night we decided to stay at a beautiful country inn I found online called Villa Paggi run by a warm and friendly Italian couple. We were famished when we checked into the inn and asked the innkeeper what her favorite restaurant in the area was. The woman mentioned she had just made some reservations for a group at a farmhouse up the hill for a fixed price dinner, and we said that sounded great to us.

"Well," she said looking at us with concern, "how much do you eat?" No one had ever asked me that before. I was confused and slightly insulted, as I was known back home to out-eat every guy I every dated.

"What do you mean?"

"Well," she said in her Italian accent, "some woman do not like to eat a lot. And it is such a pity, such a pity, because this man prepare so much food, and to see it go to waste—it would be such a shame."

I stood a little bit taller. "I will not disappoint you," I replied, and she made the call.

After having a glass of red wine on our patio overlooking

mountains and the ocean in the distance, we began the trek up a steep hill toward a pink house.

"I'm either out of shape, or the wine is getting to me," my Dad said panting.

"It's the wine." I knew my Dad was a lightweight, and he actually took pride in it, often announcing to my brother and I whenever he was buzzed off two thirds of a beer.

As we approached the porch of the pink house we were greeted by Roberto, a doughy man with a thick black mustache who was the epitome of a jolly, round Italian chef. His sidekick was a beautiful blonde girl from Ukraine named Olga, and together they created what was—and I'm certain will remain—the best meal of my life. The courses for our dinner were as follows:

1. Fresh bread with Roberto's own pressed olive oil
2. An array of different salamis and prosciuttos
3. Mushrooms in truffle oil
4. A quiche-like pie made from potatoes and beans
5. Mushroom salad
6. More mushrooms
7. Pasta sacs filled with cheese made from scratch by Olga
8. An entire chicken
9. Cheese drizzled in local honey
10. Panna Cotta
11. Limoncello shots

I had never eaten so many mushrooms in my life, and after hearing tales of my friends eating mushrooms during their study abroad trips to Amsterdam, I wondered if this feeling of euphoria could be some sort of high. But no—it was purely a food-induced nirvana, and all of these courses cost us just 25 euro. My Dad and I sat in silent appreciation for what we had just taken in. Roberto explained that he felt an obligation to serve all this food at a fair price, since it made him feel good and served as his fulfillment. Everything was prepared at his pink home, cooked onsite with ingredients from his own gardens along with local farms, and served on his porch overlooking this town by the sea. The meal also included unlimited wine, which my Dad indulged in a little more than I did.

"Here comes Olga with another course!" he yelled. "Bravo! Bravo! Bellissimo!" Olga nodded, and scurried back into the kitchen.

I had the foresight to wear spandex for this meal so my pants could expand in partnership with my waist, but I actually thought they might rip by the eighth course. Roberto told me I looked like a girl from one of Botticelli's paintings with my blonde curly hair and round face. At the time I was only familiar with Botticelli's "Birth of Venus" piece depicting a curvy nude Venus standing in a giant open clamshell, so I wasn't sure what to make of the compliment. Roberto and I continued chatting, slipping from Italian to English to Italian, since he and I only knew a few phrases here and there of each other's language. When we told Roberto this was the best meal we ever had in our lives, Roberto gave us a quintessential response. He just smiled, shrugged and said, "normal".

When I hugged and said goodbye to Roberto, I felt like I was leaving a lifelong friend. I said I'd be back someday, and I meant it. Following my lead, my Dad hugged Roberto, then Olga, and then all six of the Australians sitting next to us. After he had gone through the entire group and went back to hug the same Australian man he started with, I knew it was time to go, and down the hill we staggered.

I wanted to lie on the pavement and log roll down the hill back to the Inn. "Wow, my butt is so sore," I said to my Dad in between slow steps. "Must be from all the walking we've done." After five minutes the feeling completely faded, and I made the pathetic realization that the soreness was not from exercise, but was the result of sitting and eating for three hours straight.

The next morning the Innkeepers served us a large breakfast of breads, cakes, and fruits under the bright sun on the patio. My Dad spilt his coffee all over his plate before even taking his first bite of food, and I knew he was struggling.

"God, I am so hung over," he said.

"I can see that. But I thought you only had a few glasses of wine?"

"I know. And I feel like I went to a frat party last night. Drinking is the devil. You should stop completely."

I wasn't sure why it seemed *I* was being reprimanded for *his* hangover, but I knew he was in rough shape. Two Blue Moons was all it ever took for my Dad to spiral out of sobriety and become totally intoxicated, and consequently he rarely had more than one drink. It fascinated my brother and I the way he couldn't handle booze, especially since he had such crazy college stories, so I found it impossible that these stories could have been a result of one or two beers as he claimed.

* * *

We made the long drive through the mountains of Volastra, yet again just narrowly avoiding death by cliff fall. Volastra was a little village on a mountain high above the sea in Cinque Terre, a famous portion of the Italian Riviera known to have some of the best hiking in the world. I secured an apartment for rent on a weird Italian website I found and Google translated into English.

We met the apartment owner, Marta, an Italian woman who spoke no English, in a parking lot located outside the village since it could not be directly accessed by car. Marta led us to her apartment, chatting with us a mile a minute in Italian. Thank God what little Italian I learned studying in Florence for four months surfaced in this situation, for I could vaguely follow while my Dad looked completely lost. He was still feeling the misery of his hangover and responded the way he did with everyone in Europe he couldn't understand—he would smile, nod incessantly, and avoid eye contact.

Marta finished cleaning the apartment while my Dad and I unpacked. During our hazy Italian conversation, I thought she mentioned something about her husband Marco giving us a tour.

"Dad, I think Marta said her husband Marco is coming over to give us a tour of some sort."

"No. No tours," he said shaking his head. "I'm so hung over and need to nap." He was visibly agitated and exhausted, and I didn't want to press the issue. It had also just begun to rain and thunder, so I figured a tour wouldn't be possible anyway.

Thirty minutes later the rain had stopped and Marta entered my room, speaking loud and fast again. I had to ask her to repeat what she was saying, and sensing my confusion, Marta motioned for my Dad and I to follow her. She led us out of the apartment and back to the parking lot where an older man with white wispy hair was leaning against his car waiting for us. This was her husband Marco, who greeted us excitedly and gestured for us to get into his car. Neither my Dad nor I were expecting this, so when my Dad put the pieces together that we were to get in Marco's car, he started to freak out.

"Kristin!" he yelled as I climbed into the passenger seat. "Where are we going?"

"Dad, I don't know."

"Well ask him, I don't want to tour for hours. I am way too tired."

I turned to look at Marco, opened my mouth and paused when I saw his eager smile earnestly beaming back at me. I turned to my Dad who was stubbornly standing outside the car, and then, as sternly and calmly as I could, told my Dad to get in the car.

"No," he said, acting like a difficult toddler.

In that moment we had a total role reversal, and I wasn't backing down.

"Dad, get in the car. He's excited to take us somewhere, let's just go and see what happens."

My Dad did not look pleased with me. But something in my tone must have registered with him, and to my surprise, cranky-pants got in the back seat. Not understanding a word of English, Marco looked perplexed and must have thought this was the most bizarre father-daughter dynamic he'd ever seen.

Marco was extremely loquacious, chatting with me in Italian the entire ride while my Dad sulked in the back seat like a grouchy and defeated kid. Admittedly I could barely comprehend what Marco was saying, but he spoke with such enthusiasm and zeal I enjoyed every minute of our talk, shaking my head gravely whenever he shook his, laughing whenever he laughed. I was able to manage the conversation and never heard a peep from my Dad behind me, still too hung over from his two or three glasses of red wine to even acknowledge his surroundings.

Marco took us to his personal wine cellar built into a hill of vineyards, unlocked the door and led us into a small dark room. He then handed us two glasses, walked over to a wooden barrel and signaled us to pour some of the white wine from the nozzle. I guzzled mine down effortlessly while my Dad looked like he was sipping on gasoline. Marco then grabbed a bottle of an amber colored liquid and mimicked the movements of someone guzzling the bottle then passing out and pointed to my Dad, which made all of us laugh, and I could see my Dad's mood lifting. "Medicine," Marco said as he pointed to the bottle before pouring a small amount into three glasses. With a bit of hesitancy, I took a tiny sip, expecting to taste something strong and fiery. Instead it tasted sweet and crisp. My Dad put the glass to his lips but promptly put it back down again after turning a shade of green. Marco looked confused but moved right on to his barrel of olive oil for sampling.

Marco was animated, outgoing, and fit. He was a professional gardener who loved and understood the land, and my Dad and I were energized by his infectiously upbeat demeanor. We walked outside the cellar and Marco pulled a bunch of what looked like little oranges the size of quarters off some trees. He ate them with the skin on and we did the same. Tiny bursts of juice flooded my mouth, and I heard my Dad let out a "Wow" before climbing back into Marco's car, all the while never knowing where we were going.

We parked on the side of the road next to a hill and began climbing walls of rock, or terraces, as much of the agriculture of Cinque Terre is built into hillsides. Marco stopped and shook a tree and nuts came tumbling down from the branches, and my Dad began to watch his every move as if he were some sort of wizard. Marco gathered the nuts, broke the shells between two rocks and handed us the insides.

As we meandered through rows of cherry tomatoes, my Dad tried desperately to converse with him. "HOW YOU GET NO BUGS?" he screamed, talking to Marco as if he were deaf and sheer volume would overcome the language barrier. Not knowing the Italian word for "bug" I couldn't help him out here, but it was evident my Dad was a new man, thoroughly impressed with Marco's green thumb and enjoying every minute of this garden tour.

Farther up the mountain we met two men working on a shiny metal rail that stretched as far as the eye could see up the mountain's side. "What on earth is this for?" my Dad asked curiously as we both craned our necks upward.

"It must be for getting up and down the hillside," I said.

But the rail-cart was just a few wooden boards and it seemed impossible that it could safely hold people, so I assumed it was for transporting grapes.

Marco walked over to a little shed, ducked inside and then reappeared carrying a large jug of gasoline. He straddled the motor in the front, poured in the gas, and motioned my Dad and I to sit in the wooden car, facing backward toward the ocean and valley below. I couldn't believe it—here we were on a steep mountain about to climb aboard what was essentially a rickety roller coaster with no side rails and nothing to strap us in place or to prevent us from falling. For the hundredth time during the trip, I thought of death by cliff fall. If the brakes ever malfunctioned, we would careen down the mountain exactly as we would on a runaway train.

Being fully aware of this, we climbed onto the car anyway, propelled by the uncertainty of this adventure with Marco. The trip was pushing us out of our usual comfort zones, and we went with the flow, open to new experiences.

The ascent was thrilling and beautiful, and we passed endless lush green vineyards as the sun broke through the clouds and illuminated the surrounding hills. We halted and hopped off to meander rows of Marco's grapevines, stopping to sit under their shade and break off bushels of grapes to eat. We got back on the track and Marco drove our little train to dizzying heights. Higher and higher we went, and we craned our heads around trying to see the top of the mountain, silently praying Marco knew what he was doing. My Dad whispered to me, "if he runs out of fuel, we're as good as dead."

"Thank you for that bit of uplifting news," I answered. But I had to agree, thinking that even if Marco had brakes on this contraption, nothing could safely hold our weight on such an incline. I sat back and tried to enjoy the view.

Finally the rail leveled off and our cart came to a halt at the top of the mountain. Marco jumped off and motioned us to follow, and we walked a narrow path around the summit to the west side. What we saw next made me want to stay here forever. Nestled into the hillside, almost level with the clouds was a small one room stone cabin with a large patio and two chairs overlooking all of Cinque Terre. "Paradisio," Marco said, and he was right. My Dad and I each took a seat, gaping in awe at the landscape of sparkling emerald water dancing behind bright, multicolored villages. Marco ventured to a few trees and came back with a handful of fresh pulled figs and apples, and the three of us sat and chewed in silent appreciation, feeling joy and gratitude to be in this special place.

On the way down the mountain we stopped at another garden of Marco's where he picked up fresh peppers, onions, tomatoes, and basil. Then we drove to another village of Cinque Terre to explore the streets, and in a ten minute period, Marco exchanged warm greetings with at least thirty friends. It was incredible the way everyone knew each other here. He then took us to a supermercato, which was essentially the size of a small bedroom that had been lined with groceries. After we picked up spaghetti and olive oil, Marco drove us back to the parking lot near our apartment where we hugged and thanked him. I had a better grasp of Italian after spending four hours conversing with him than I did after four months studying in Italy. *This has been the perfect vacation,* I thought. We had no major bumps in the road (well, figuratively, that is). What could go wrong?

Once at the apartment we decided to cook our spaghetti and make a sauce with the fresh ingredients Marco had given us. After wasting ten minutes trying to figure out how to turn on the gas stove, we found a dial behind the cooktop, turned the nozzle for the burner and lit the gas with a match. On top of the four burners was a thick sheet of glass which we assumed was the surface to cook on. After the gas was ablaze we placed a large pot of water on the glass over the burner and set about searching the cabinets for plates.

I was reaching for two white plates when the room exploded with a deafening BOOM! A million fragments of shattered glass filled the air of the small kitchen.

I stood stunned and wide-eyed with my jaw hanging open, ears ringing and heart pounding. After what felt like an eternity in this condition, I came to my senses and whipped my head toward my Dad, whose face mirrored my sheer terror and confusion. We stood like this for a full minute, neither of us able to speak or move. Had someone shot a gun through a window? Had the apartment exploded? Were we even alive?

I put my hand to my face expecting it to be covered with blood, and my Dad did the same, only he was feeling his entire head as if surprised to find it still attached to his neck. There was no blood on my hand or any that I could see on my Dad, but little crystals of glass fell from our hair and shoulders like dandruff. "Holy shit," were the only words spoken in the long moments that followed those seconds of chaos. It was an absolute miracle that we weren't injured. Both of us had just turned our bodies to be facing away from the stove of this tiny kitchen when the glass exploded.

It took us far too long to realize and process that what happened was actually quite simple: we were idiots. The glass sheath covering the burners was just a protective cover meant to be lifted off the stovetop before cooking. We had left it down and it had heated to the point of bursting like a bomb, sending shards of glass across every inch of the kitchen.

We swept up innumerable tiny pieces of glass in complete silence. Finally my Dad spoke up.

"We are the luckiest people on the planet. I honestly thought there was a gas leak and the apartment was exploding." Then he paused and said, "We will have to tell Marta and Marco, but not tonight. We have to think about how to break the bad news." Since my Dad couldn't speak Italian, I realized what he was really saying: *you will have to tell them, so think about what you're going to say.*

* * *

The next day we hiked an hour to the neighboring village of Corniglia. Upon arrival, we rewarded ourselves with gelato drizzled in honey and were sitting on a bench in an alley enjoying our snack when a small, blue painted sign caught my eye. It read "spiaggia" with an arrow pointing to a narrow opening between the alley walls. We couldn't resist and followed a steep series of stone steps that led to a breathtaking secluded beach in a rocky cliff cove encased by crystal clear blue waters. The ocean was rough and choppy, but we put on our masks and snorkels anyway and dove into a pool of little silver fish, the smallest ones following us wherever we swam, staying within a few inches of our bodies. We sunned and rested our legs there among local sunbathers before we hiked back up to Corniglia and devoured a pesto pizza like wolves.

It was an absolutely picturesque day as the seas calmed, the sun was shining and the sky clear and blue. Happy hikers passed in abundance, eager like us to take on the day. But our energy began to wane as we hiked the rocky, zigzag path connecting Corniglia to Vernazza. The sun's blaze was harsh as my tired legs began to shake, and my Dad had to stop every ten minutes to pee. Feeling exhausted as well, he had wanted to turn back. But just as

I had done during the prior day's trip with Marco, I implored him to suck it up, adding, "C'mon Dad, who knows what awaits us in the next town!" He wasn't buying it and sat on a stone step, suggesting we be like the locals and take a siesta. I decided not to tell him siesta was actually Spanish, but I found another way to get him back on his feet by reminding him of all the mountains we climbed in New England throughout the years, saying surely he wasn't getting so old that he couldn't keep up with me.

Two exhausting hours later Vernazza was in sight, and we could hear sporadic cheering in the distance coming from the village. We spotted a crowd of people gathered in the marina and headed there to discover a polo match occurring in the bay. Spectators sat scattered along the jetty with their legs dangling into the water, and we joined them. The referee was an older man completely in white—white t-shirt, white pants, white shoes, and white hair. He stood behind us pacing back and forth along the jetty, blowing his whistle vehemently.

I was immediately intrigued by the sport and the men playing it. I had read in a Cosmo magazine that polo players had the most athletic bodies because their sport required them to tread water for hours on end, and having been a witness, I can attest that this is indeed an irrefutable fact. After an hour of watching—and coming to the disappointing realization that my future husband was likely not among the polo players in the water before me—I was ready to take the train back. But my Dad was enjoying the polo match far too much, cheering and even shouting advice to the players. He insisted we stay another few minutes, and to my embarrassment, began cheering for the visiting team as the locals around us glared in our direction. When he shouted to a player, "You need to shoot more often, forget about passing every time you get the ball!" I grabbed him by the hand and hauled him out of there, remarking that it was time for our second gelato of the day.

The next morning we packed our bags and waited for Marta and Marco to show up and collect our keys, and I had no idea what I was going to say about our little cooking accident. How do you explain to someone who doesn't speak your language that you blew up their stove out of sheer stupidity?

We were cleaning the dirt trail left by my Dad's sneakers and picking up a few remaining shards of glass when Marta knocked on the door. My Dad let her in, and thinking his ninth grade Spanish might be understood by her, said, "Poco...little... problemo," holding his hands before him with his palms up. Marta cocked her head sensing trouble. He did a little pivot, and pointing at me, quickly croaked, "Kristin will explain."

I was caught off guard, but managed to mumble an apology while pointing to the stove. Marta transformed from bubbly landlord to heated Italian woman and went off on a rant talking at the speed of light, her arms flailing wildly. She bent down over the stove and carefully observed what little was left of the glass surface. I tried explaining to her that we were boiling water when the glass exploded, and feeling left out, my Dad stepped in and made an exploding sound with his mouth while throwing his hands up in the air. I rolled my eyes at his charade attempt and looked back at Marta, saying I'm sorry in Italian over and over. Marta then apologized back, saying she would need to collect fifty euro for the damage. It was less expensive than we thought it would be, and I think Marta genuinely felt sorry for *us*, probably pitying our ignorance.

* * *

That afternoon was spent driving back through France as we had planned to end our trip in Nice. I booked the most reasonably priced hotel I could find online, which was listed as a "Premiere" hotel and was situated next to the airport, so I thought it had to be legitimate.

When we entered the closet-sized lobby, it took me some time to realize that there was no traditional front desk, but rather a computer on a podium-like piece of furniture. After ringing the bell several times, a young girl appeared and checked us in.

We found our room on the third floor, and what was on the other side of the door can only be described as something you might find in the cabin of a small, small ship. My Dad and I expressed this thought simultaneously. Instead of two double beds, the room housed two single bunk beds stacked on top of one another against the left wall. On the right wall was a small bureau supporting a large old TV. The bathroom looked exactly like the inside of a Port-A-Potty, and a plastic toilet was stuck to the wall next to a sink made for a hobbit and a thin shower built only for a person who had first been pressed flat like a panini. The room was listed a "sea view" room, so the next thing I did was walk up to the room's only circular window which was the exact size of my head. In the distance was an extremely long runway, with only the faintest glimmer of the sea behind it miles in the distance.

It was late in the evening when we arrived, so we decided to take a walk along the street in an effort to find some food. It took about ten seconds into the walk to realize we were in an extremely sketchy area. This was not at all how I pictured our stay in Nice, especially after we entered a shop that reeked of tobacco, where five men smoking cigarettes stood still and glared at us like we were trespassers as we picked up yogurt, cheese and two bananas. I felt paranoid as they continued puffing smoke in skeptical silence, watching our every move as if they recognized us from a recent WANTED poster.

Things got worse from there. We had just closed the door of our miniature cabin and peeled open our yogurts when a number of male voices could be heard shouting from the hallway. This was followed by an incessant banging and slamming of doors, which went on for twenty disturbing minutes. It was 9 p.m., and soon there were rapid knocks on our door and several male voices harshly yelling to us in a language I couldn't discern. I was attempting to read in the top bunk, and without exchanging words or glances, I could sense how alarmed my Dad was from the bunk below.

"Wait just a second," he said as he rose from his bed and headed towards the violent banging and yelling. "Who is it?" he demanded, both of us looking at the door bewildered. Then the door handle started jiggling rapidly, and I grew more nervous and concerned. When his question was met with more barbarous, indecipherable shouting, he fired back.

"Quiet!"

My Dad yelled in a voice I hadn't heard in many, many years. I had no idea whose voice it was—it belonged to an authoritative, commanding, intimidating person, and in that moment my Dad became unrecognizable to me. Suddenly he wasn't my 5'8" and 150lb down-to-earth father, but someone who could seriously kick your ass. A friend of his once told me a story of how he punched a guy at a Patriots game who had asked to borrow his binoculars and wouldn't give them back. A fight ensued and stadium security dragged my Dad away in handcuffs. The message here is that NO ONE messes with Mike Tougias and his binoculars. No one.

The shouting on the other side of the door only grew louder. My Dad broke the tension by turning to me, saying, "We should have stayed in the nursing home next door."

"Yea," I scoffed from the top bunk where I sat frozen, although a little confused by his choice of lodging. "Anything would be better than this."

"No, I'm being serious. I spoke in New Hampshire a month ago, and rather than a hotel I stayed in a nursing home. It wasn't great but it was free, and no one tried to break into my room." While I was a little alarmed that he had actually stayed in a nursing home, I would have welcomed the same shelter that moment.

Among the many shortcomings of this hotel room was the fact that there was only a single lock on the doorknob and no peephole. We went to call the front desk but there was no phone in the room. More rapid jiggling of the door handle ensued, and my Dad reached out to open it. "Dad!" I barked. "Don't open the door. It's not the manager—no hotel personnel would be trying to break into the room like that." Realizing I was probably right, he backed away. I was certain we were going to be held at gunpoint and robbed at any moment. After all, we were staying in a two star hotel with no front desk in a sketchy part of France.

Whoever was outside the door now started kicking it, apparently trying to break the lock.

"We've got to arm ourselves," my Dad said, while turning away from the door. He reached into his bag and pulled out a half-empty red wine bottle. He then went to a tiny closet with the capacity to hold a single winter coat, drew a metal hanger and handed it to me in the top bunk. "For defense," he stated firmly as I took it from him. I inspected the frail hanger. *How can I possibly fight off five men with this?*

It reminded me of a family trip we had taken to St. John that same year, where my Dad instructed Brian and I to keep some sort of weapon by our bedside as we were staying in a remotely located home. My Dad's weapon of choice? A knife and a cutting board.

"Are you planning on serving our intruders cheese?" I had asked sarcastically.

"No" he replied. "The cutting board is my shield."

He gave me a rolling pin and Brian a spatula.

Now, my Dad held the wine bottle out in front of him and slashed it through the air like a sword. "Aha!" he said proudly. "Even with a gun they won't be able to get past this bottle."

I highly doubted that.

I remained on edge for the next two hours, staked out in my top bunk like a navy seal perched at a lookout as I clutched the clothes hanger. Loud, startling bangs from aggressive pounding and door slamming made me jump every ten seconds. My Dad was on edge too, and to pass the time he occasionally went to the little circular window.

"Hooker's still there," he said matter-of-factly. "Nope—wait—a car's just pulled up. She's getting in." He had been giving me the play by play of a prostitute's every move for the last half hour like a commentator of an NFL game. "Yup. She's gone," he said sadly. "I wish her the best of luck."

This was certainly an unanticipated view, quite different from the beautiful beach setting that I had envisioned would lay beyond the windows of our "sea view" room.

"I'm going downstairs to request a room change," my Dad said, nearing the end of his patience.

"No!" I called out dramatically. "It isn't safe!" But the noises had subsided and we had been graced with a few minutes of silence.

"I think they're gone—for now," he said. "Stay here."

I held my breath as he exited—weapon in hand—and I said a silent prayer, thinking this may be the last time I'd ever see him again. I was so relieved when he returned five minutes later. "Come on," he said. "We're moving rooms." We gathered our things in a hurry like two people who had just been told they must immediately leave the country. I opened the door slowly, peeked out, and made a run for the elevator in my pajamas clutching my belongings. In my sprint to the end of the hallway I passed eight teenagers engaged in a heated game of soccer in the hallway, their shouting sounding exactly like the men thought to have been breaking into our room.

When the elevator doors closed, my Dad and I looked at each other, having made the simultaneous realization that these were the "intruders" we were so petrified of and prepared to fight for the last three hours. They were harmless students on a field trip, the soccer game in the hallway being the root of all the commotion, and our room just happened to be in the center of it. They probably mistook our door for belonging to some of their friends, and that's why they were pounding on it so hard. I felt so silly, and upon this concurrent realization in the elevator, my Dad and I erupted into such a fit of screaming laughter I thought we were going to pass out. We laughed the entire way to our newly assigned room and laughed even harder when we opened the door and entered an even *smaller* room than before, with two cot-like single beds that smelled like something had died inside their thin, lumpy mattresses.

* * *

On the plane ride home the next morning we reminisced and cracked up recounting the sweating cheese, his three glasses of wine hangover, the unsafe ride up the mountain of Cinque Terre, the stove explosion, and the incident in the "sea-view" room.

When I asked my Dad if he had any food, he rummaged through his backpack to see what he could dig up. "Hmm, I don't think so. Wait a minute—here's something," he said, pulling out a small Snickers bar whose rapper had been partially torn, its contents turned to dust. We again began laughing so hard that every single person within earshot turned to look at the father-daughter duo gone mad.

* * *

This was the last period of my life living at home, under the same roof with my father. I would soon move to New York City and begin working full time. Not knowing where my life would take me next, I was so thankful for this trip, and for all the amazing trips I had with my Dad. The many cringe-worthy moments throughout those 22 years made us closer than ever, as we had grown to be incredible partners, travel companions and best friends.

* * *

A Dad's View

Life just gets stranger and stranger as the years pass. Through Kristin's entire teenage years she either was dragged on family trips against her will, or she came along so as not to hurt my feelings. And here she was—a young adult who could do anything she wished with her vacation time—choosing to travel with Dear Old Dad, making the trip to France and Italy such a wonderful success.

It felt like just yesterday I was beginning my writing career, a young Dad researching hiking trails with an infant Kristin in my backpack. Never did I think I'd see the day she would be the one planning our vacations, and that I'd be following her advice on how to thrive in a foreign country.

* * *

With Kristin's adult life just beginning, I was so thankful for our relationship and all our journeys together. There is no such thing as a bad trip when you travel with someone you love.

Author Programs

Michael and Kristin Tougias are available for presentations where they discuss the writing of The Cringe Chronicles, share images from their misadventures, and use humor to tell their story – even when they disagree.

Organizations can contact Michael at michaeltougias@yahoo.com or through his website at www.michaeltougias.com.

Visit his author Facebook page at Michael J. Tougias.

Michael also gives presentations on all his books to groups, businesses and students across the country.

Also by Michael J. Tougias

Derek's Gift: A True Story of Love, Courage, and Lessons Learned
(co-author Buck Harris)

There's A Porcupine In My Outhouse:
The Vermont Misadventures of a Mountain Man Wannabe

Rescue of the Bounty:
A True Story of Disaster and Survival in Super-storm Sandy
(co-author Douglas Campbell)

A Storm Too Soon:
A True Story of Disaster, Survival and an Incredible Rescue

Overboard! A True Blue-Water Odyssey of Disaster and Survival

Fatal Forecast: An Incredible True Story of Disaster and Survival at Sea

Ten Hours Until Dawn:
The True Story of Heroism and Tragedy Aboard the Can Do

The Finest Hours:
The True Story of the U.S. Coast Guard's Most Daring Sea Rescue
(co-author Casey Sherman)

Until I Have No Country: A Novel of King Philip's Indian War

King Philip's War: The History and Legacy of America's Forgotten Conflict
(co-author Eric Schultz)

BLACK ROSE

writing™

CPSIA information can be obtained at www.ICGtesting.com
Printed in the USA
BVOW08s1210120315

391390BV00004B/11/P